I0824963

VEGETABLES
THE ITALIAN WAY

VEGETABLES THE ITALIAN WAY

TURNING SIMPLE AND FRESH INTO EXTRAORDINARY

Giulia Scarpaleggia

Photographs by Tommaso Galli

ARTISAN | NEW YORK

Library of Congress Cataloging-in-Publication Data
Names: Scarpaleggia, Giulia author | Galli, Tommaso photographer
Title: Vegetables the Italian way / Giulia Scarpaleggia ; photographs by Tommaso Galli.
Description: New York, NY : Artisan, [2026] | Includes index.
Identifiers: LCCN 2025026566 | ISBN 9781648294679 (hardcover); ISBN 9781648294693 (ebook)
Subjects: LCSH: Cooking, Italian | Cooking (Vegetables) | LCGFT: Cookbooks
Classification: LCC TX723 .S3558 2026 | DDC 641.6/50945—dc23 /eng/20250702
LC record available at https://lccn.loc.gov/2025026566

Design by Jan Derevjanik

Artisan books may be purchased in bulk for business, educational, or promotional use. For information, please contact your local bookseller or the Hachette Book Group Special Markets Department at special.markets@hbgusa.com.

Published by Artisan,
an imprint of Workman Publishing,
a division of Hachette Book Group, Inc.
1290 Avenue of the Americas
New York, NY 10104
artisanbooks.com

Printed in China (TLF) on responsibly sourced paper

First printing, February 2026

10 9 8 7 6 5 4 3 2 1

In loving memory of
Nonna Marcella—
forever linked to the scent
of green tomato leaves,
the deeply savory taste
of stewed green beans,
and your unmatched
eggplant parmigiana.
You will live on in every
gesture I make in the
kitchen, in every recipe I
share with our family.

CONTENTS

introduction

A VEGETABLE LOVE AFFAIR

Italians have a gift for making vegetables shine. It's about simplicity, balance, and an instinctive understanding of flavor—coaxing the best out of each ingredient with a few thoughtful touches. A drizzle of olive oil, a sprinkle of salt, maybe a squeeze of lemon, or a handful of fresh herbs can transform even the humblest vegetable into something memorable. This deep-rooted practice of simplicity comes from Italy's long agricultural history, where cooks learned to make the most of what the land provided and the traditions of cucina povera emphasize simplicity, resourcefulness, and affordability.

Italy's connection to the land runs deep. For generations, families have grown their own food—not necessarily in sprawling gardens but in small plots, shared fields, or even a handful of tomato plants nurtured in pots. Today, this practice endures. Markets brim with seasonal produce, and more people maintain a home garden as a way to reconnect to traditions that once defined everyday life.

This respect for vegetables shapes how Italians cook them, celebrating them for what they are rather than masking them, whether it's roasting zucchini until caramelized, slow-cooking onions into a sweet jam, or preserving the season's last artichokes in olive oil. The result is a cuisine where vegetables aren't an afterthought or relegated to a supporting role but are the heart of the meal.

Turn these pages to learn how Italian home cooks make the most of vegetables year-round. While seasonal vegetables often take center stage in home cooking, they don't always shine when you're dining out in trattorias and restaurants. One of the questions I'm asked most frequently when I host my cooking classes is, Where are the vegetables? A typical Tuscan restaurant menu might offer a simple lettuce salad, a few slices of tomato, or sautéed spinach, but rarely anything more. Yet our markets are bursting with fresh seasonal vegetables. Even in the smallest neighborhood stalls where vendors sell pots and pans, aprons, and roasted chicken, you'll find crates of freshly harvested produce. If trattorias and restaurants give you quite an accurate idea of what we eat at home in terms of pasta and meat courses, the same can't be said for vegetables. In homes across Italy, vegetables are woven into every part of the meal, from appetizers and pasta sauces to side dishes and hearty main courses.

Walk through any neighborhood market, and you'll see why. Seasonal vegetables are the backbone of everyday cooking, paired instinctively with pantry staples like extra-virgin olive oil, aged cheeses, legumes, and grains. Italian home cooking is less about following recipes to the letter and more about cooking with what's available: what's in season, what looks good at the market, or what's ripe in the garden. That's where the magic happens.

Eating seasonally and locally has always been one of the cornerstones of Italian cucina povera, which was a necessity before becoming a trend. This, paired with a creative approach featuring vegetables as the hero of a dish, have resulted in some of Italy's most beloved recipes.

A TUSCAN LIFE

In many ways, this book is a tribute to a cooking philosophy that I inherited from my grandmother, who could turn a handful of vegetables into the most comforting of meals. I've been lucky enough to grow up and live in a house in the Tuscan countryside, surrounded by an olive grove and a large vegetable garden, that is a constant source of inspiration for how I cook and how I live, attuned to the seasons. In my family, vegetables are something to celebrate at their peak or to preserve for the colder months. Either way, they become the focal point of our meals.

When I cook at home for my husband and daughter and plan our weekly menu, the first question is always, What is in season? How will I cook what I just bought at the market? How do I make the most of the glut of zucchini the vegetable garden is giving us right now? A sheet pan of roasted vegetables (see page 186) is one of the most common weeknight dishes that we eat, easily turned into a meal with some crumbled cheese on top and a slice of sourdough bread alongside. In summer, a green bean and potato salad (see page 24), maybe enriched with hard-boiled eggs and basil, is a dish that solves many a meal. There are days when I crave hot soups, others when I want to see the grill marks on a pepper or an eggplant, cherishing their smoky flavor.

I've been a cooking class teacher for fifteen years. In the cooking classes my husband and I host in the Tuscan countryside, seasonal vegetables are always at the heart of the menu. Our guests often arrive expecting pasta to be the star ingredient but leave with a deeper understanding of how vegetables shape the rhythm of everyday Italian cooking. A visit to the local market is often the highlight of the class and a hands-on way to experience the creativity and simplicity that define an Italian meal.

THE RECIPES

The recipes in this book are a celebration of cucina casalinga, Italian home cooking. You will find recipes that have been inspired by iconic Italian dishes or capitalize on the bounty of a region or a city. They showcase ingredients that tell a geographical, cultural, or political story, and flavors that pique your imagination and re-create a vivid sense of place. Think about the Sicilian caponata (see page 143) studded with olives and capers, the slow-stewed Roman artichokes (see page 43), or even the green stuffed cascioni from Romagna (see page 209), where a piadina is folded over, sealed, and stuffed with a filling of garlic-infused spinach.

This book is organized by cooking method—from Tossed and Stirred to Braised, Boiled, and Stewed to Baked and Roasted to Stuffed, and even includes Preserved and Sweetened—because the best way to celebrate vegetables the Italian way is through simple techniques that amplify their natural qualities. This isn't just a structural choice; it illustrates how Italian home cooks approach vegetables: with respect for their natural character and an understanding of how the right cooking method can unlock their full potential.

Within each chapter, recipes are arranged seasonally, moving from spring's delicate greens to the hearty squashes and root vegetables of winter. Rather than a strict division into separate seasons, there's a natural flow from one season to the next, mirroring how ingredients follow each other in market stalls and onto the table. It reflects the rhythm of Italian home cooking, where the end of one harvest seamlessly gives way to the next.

Where helpful, each recipe includes serving suggestions that capture the Italian way of eating. You'll find indications for antipasti (appetizers), meant to open the meal with small bites or shareable plates; primi piatti (first courses), typically pasta, rice, or gnocchi dishes that form the heart of an Italian meal; and secondi (main courses), where vegetables take the spotlight as satisfying stand-alone dishes. These suggestions can help you create balanced menus or simply choose how to enjoy each recipe based on the occasion.

The recipes take into account the contemporary need for a more sustainable way of eating, too. While this isn't a vegetarian or vegan cookbook, many recipes are, or can easily be adapted to suit those diets with a few tweaks. They show you how to incorporate vegetables into your daily meals, how to joyfully eat more of them, and how to make them the protagonists of your menus.

When possible, recipes will include tips on how to prep the vegetables and how to freeze and store the different preparations or the final dish. Many dishes can be made ahead, or partially made ahead, to accommodate the busy lives of those who still want to cook a wholesome meal for their weeknight dinners.

Along with the classic recipes like My Grandma's Eggplant Parmigiana (page 170) and Stuffed Cabbage Rolls (page 211), there are also recipes born from listening to old nonnas queuing at the market, speaking with farmers, or those created on a whim after a market haul. All these recipes exalt seasonality and have a strong Italian accent: simple ingredients and preparations, a preference for good extra-virgin olive oil, and a bouquet of fresh herbs. This is how I cook on a daily basis, so here you will find many of those recipes that are part of my culinary repertoire, such as Pasta with Broccoli (page 83) and Tomato Tonnato (page 20).

So think beyond the usual carbonara and pizza and you'll uncover some recipe gems that may become your new favorite veg-forward meals, inspiring you to cook with creativity and delight while putting vegetables at the center of your table.

TurboDaily
Amélie

TOSS
ED &
STIR
RED

Bright, crisp salads and simply dressed vegetables showcase peak-season freshness. Here raw and lightly cooked vegetables take center stage, paired with vibrant dressings that amplify their natural flavors.

asparagi con la salsa delle puntarelle

ASPARAGUS SALAD WITH ANCHOVY DRESSING

Serves 4 to 6 as an appetizer

- 1 pound/450 g asparagus
- ½ cup/120 ml extra-virgin olive oil
- ¼ cup/60 ml apple cider vinegar
- 2 tablespoons fresh lemon juice
- 8 oil-packed anchovy fillets, chopped
- 2 garlic cloves, smashed and peeled
- Fine sea salt and freshly ground black pepper

Fresh, slender asparagus at the peak of its season is best eaten raw, or thinly sliced and tossed with a punchy vinaigrette. Use this dressing inspired by one of Rome's most iconic dishes: puntarelle salad. Made from an emulsion of garlic, olive oil, anchovies, lemon juice, and vinegar, the pungent dressing pairs perfectly with the thinly shaved asparagus. It's the kind of dish that begs for crusty bread to mop up every last drop.

Snap off the hard woody ends of the asparagus. Rinse the spears, then slice them on the bias ⅛ inch/3 mm thick. Save the tips and slice them lengthwise. Collect all the pieces in a bowl.

In the cup of an immersion blender (or in a stand blender), combine the olive oil, vinegar, lemon juice, 4 of the anchovies, and the garlic. Blend until you get a creamy, thick dressing. Adjust the seasoning with salt, if needed, and add several grinds of pepper.

Pour the dressing over the asparagus in the bowl, toss, add the remaining anchovies, and serve immediately.

NOTE: If you have leftover dressing, refrigerate it in a jar to use for salads, tossed with roasted vegetables, or as a dip for carrot and cucumber sticks.

pomodori con la salsa tonnata

TOMATO TONNATO

Serves 4 as a main course, 8 as an appetizer

- One 5- to 7-ounce/ 142 to 200 g jar or can good-quality tuna, preferably oil-packed
- ⅔ cup/ 150 g mayonnaise
- 1 anchovy fillet
- 3 tablespoons brined or salt-packed capers, rinsed, plus more for garnish
- 1 tablespoon apple cider vinegar, plus more to taste
- Kosher salt
- 4 tomatoes, your favorite type
- Fresh basil leaves
- Extra-virgin olive oil, for drizzling
- Freshly ground black pepper

This is the shortcut version of salsa tonnata, perfect for hot summer nights when you want something cooling but satisfying. The original Piedmontese recipe starts with veal, roasted until tender, whose drippings form the base of a sauce made with anchovies, egg yolks, canned tuna, brined capers, lemon juice, and olive oil. This simpler version skips the veal entirely and uses good-quality mayonnaise for a creamy, tangy dressing you can whip up in 5 minutes with a decent blender. You'll use the dressing to smother thick-sliced tomatoes—my dad prefers firm San Marzano, while I always reach for plump Cuore di Bue. Serve with slices of rustic bread to soak up all that velvety, creamy sauce.

Drain the tuna and place it in a blender or a food processor. Add the mayonnaise, anchovy, capers, and vinegar and blend until smooth. Taste and adjust the seasoning, adding some salt or another dash of vinegar if needed. (The salsa tonnata can be prepared in advance. Keep it in an airtight container in the fridge for up to 4 days.)

Cut the tomatoes into thick slices and arrange them on a platter, then spoon on the salsa tonnata. Scatter some capers and fresh basil leaves on top, drizzle with olive oil, and sprinkle with a few turns of pepper. Serve immediately.

NOTE: Leftover tomato tonnato is great on sandwiches the next day.

insalata pantesca

POTATO & TOMATO SALAD FROM PANTELLERIA

Serves 6 as a side dish

- 1 pound/450 g red-skinned potatoes (about 2 medium)
- 1 small or ½ medium red onion, thinly sliced
- ¼ cup/60 ml red wine vinegar
- ¼ cup/60 ml extra-virgin olive oil
- 1 tablespoon dried oregano
- 10 datterini, mini San Marzano, or small Roma (plum) tomatoes
- ¼ cup/20 g brined or salt-packed capers, thoroughly rinsed
- ¼ cup/30 g good-quality black or green olives, such as Taggiasca or Castelvetrano, pitted
- Handful of fresh basil leaves, torn into pieces if large
- Fine sea salt and freshly ground black pepper

The secret to an outstanding potato salad lies in two simple principles. First, choose the best ingredients: Opt for firm, waxy potatoes like Italian red-skinned varieties with yellow flesh—new potatoes are even better—and a peppery extra-virgin olive oil. Second, dress the potatoes while they're still hot. Toss them vigorously with olive oil, salt, and pepper so they can fully absorb the seasoning, creating a salad that's flavorful down to the last bite.

This insalata pantesca hails from Pantelleria, a tiny volcanic island located in the Mediterranean Sea between Sicily and Tunisia, famous for its wine and food, and especially for its capers, reputed to be the best in Italy, if not in the world.

Rinse the potatoes to remove any remaining soil. Place them in a saucepan and add water to cover. Cook the potatoes over medium heat until you can easily pierce them with the tip of a knife, about 40 minutes for medium potatoes. It might take less or longer depending on the size of your potatoes, so try to choose potatoes of all the same size.

Meanwhile, in a shallow bowl, combine the onion, vinegar, and ¼ cup/60 ml water and let stand for 30 minutes, then drain. This will tame the pungency of the onion and slightly pickle it.

In a small bowl, stir the olive oil and oregano together and let infuse for 30 minutes. The oregano will soften and release its aroma into the oil, enhancing its Mediterranean character.

Quarter or halve the tomatoes, according to their size, or cut them into about 1-inch/2.5 cm chunks if bigger. Set aside until the potatoes are done.

When the potatoes are cooked through, drain them, run them quickly under cold water, and peel them immediately.

Cut the potatoes into large pieces and add them to a large bowl. Add the tomato chunks, drained onion, capers, olives, basil leaves, and oregano–olive oil mixture. Stir well, and don't worry if the potatoes get a little bruised. This will only help the seasoning. Taste and season with salt, if needed, and pepper.

Let the potato and tomato salad sit at room temperature for at least 30 minutes, allowing enough time for all the dressing ingredients to blend before serving.

Leftovers keep well in the fridge for up to 2 days; just remember to bring the salad back to room temperature before serving.

insalata di patate e fagiolini

GREEN BEAN & POTATO SALAD

Serves 6 as a side dish

- 1 pound/450 g red-skinned potatoes
- 1 pound/450 g green beans
- Fine sea salt
- ¼ cup/60 ml extra-virgin olive oil
- ¼ cup/30 g good-quality black or green olives, like Taggiasca or Castelvetrano, pitted
- Handful of fresh basil leaves, torn into pieces if large
- Freshly ground black pepper

A cross between a green bean salad and a potato salad, this summer salad is perfumed with fresh basil and dressed with a generous drizzle of peppery extra-virgin olive oil. Make a big batch because it's the kind of dish everyone comes back to for seconds.

Rinse the potatoes to remove any remaining soil. Place them in a saucepan and add water to cover. Cook the potatoes over medium heat until you can easily pierce them with the tip of a knife, about 40 minutes for medium potatoes. It might take less or longer depending on the size of your potatoes, so try to choose potatoes of all the same size.

Meanwhile, trim the beans, rinse them, and place them in a pot of salted water over medium heat. Cook them in the boiling water until soft, about 15 minutes. Drain the beans and run them under cold water. This will stop the cooking and will preserve their bright green color.

When the potatoes are cooked through, drain them, run them quickly under cold water, and peel them immediately.

Cut the potatoes into large pieces, then add them to a large bowl. Add the beans to the potatoes and while the beans are hot, dress them with the olive oil, olives, and basil. Taste and season with salt and pepper. Let the salad sit at room temperature for at least 30 minutes, allowing enough time for all the dressing ingredients to blend. Serve the salad warm or cold.

Store leftovers in an airtight container in the fridge for up to 2 days.

insalata di cavolo nero con frutta secca tostata

EXTRA-NUTTY LACINATO KALE SALAD

Serves 6 to 8 as a side dish

½ cup/50 g walnuts

⅓ cup/45 g almonds

⅓ cup/45 g hazelnuts

4 tablespoons extra-virgin olive oil

Fine sea salt

1 pound/450 g (1 or 2 bunches) lacinato kale

1 tablespoon balsamic vinegar

Freshly ground black pepper

Chestnut honey

NOTE: Chestnut honey is one of the most unique honeys you can find in Italy. Dark and spicy, with a complex aroma and a subtly bitter aftertaste, it is the perfect honey to use in savory recipes like this salad. I love it paired with chestnut flour crepes stuffed with whipped ricotta, with an arugula salad, or drizzled over some aged pecorino cheese.

The best time to make this salad is just after the first frost of the year. The frost softens the leaves of lacinato—or Tuscan kale, what we call cavolo nero—making it sweeter and less fibrous. To bring out the full flavor of the hearty green, start by making a simple vinaigrette with extra-virgin olive oil, a pinch of salt, freshly ground black pepper, and a splash of aged aceto balsamico. Pour the dressing over the kale and toss it well, making sure to massage the leaves thoroughly. It will soften the kale even more, making it both tender and easier to digest.

Preheat the oven to 325°F/160°C.

Spread the walnuts, almonds, and hazelnuts on a small baking sheet. Drizzle with 1 tablespoon of the olive oil and sprinkle generously with salt. Toss to coat the nuts evenly, then roast until they turn golden brown and fragrant, about 20 minutes. Keep an eye on them—nuts can burn quickly. Remove from the oven and let cool completely.

Once cooled, pulse the nuts in a food processor or chop them by hand until they are roughly chopped—having some larger pieces and some finely ground bits will give the salad great texture. (The chopped nuts can be made ahead and stored in the fridge in a jar for a couple of days.)

Remove the tough stems and midribs from the kale by holding the base of the stem with one hand and stripping the leaves off with the other. Rinse the leaves thoroughly and spin them dry in a salad spinner or use kitchen towels to dry them. To thinly slice the kale, stack a few leaves together, roll them up into a cylinder, and slice crosswise into thin ribbons. (The shredded kale can be prepared in advance and kept in an airtight container in the fridge for up to a day.)

Toss the kale in a large bowl with the remaining 3 tablespoons olive oil, the balsamic vinegar, salt to taste, and a few cracks of pepper. Massage the kale with your hands to soften its fibers. Let the dressed kale sit at room temperature for about 20 minutes, then taste and season with more salt if needed.

When ready to serve, sprinkle the chopped nuts over the kale and toss everything together to distribute the crunchy seasoning. For the final touch, drizzle a bit of chestnut honey over the top, toss, and serve.

zucca in agrodolce

SWEET & SOUR SQUASH

Serves 6 as a side dish

- 2 pounds/900 g winter squash, such as Mantovana, kabocha, delicata, or butternut
- 2 medium red onions (about 1 pound/450 g total)
- ⅓ cup/80 ml extra-virgin olive oil
- 2 teaspoons fine sea salt
- ½ cup/120 ml dry white wine
- 4 tablespoons balsamic vinegar
- ¼ cup/30 g raisins
- 2 tablespoons pine nuts, toasted

Agrodolce, a combination of sweet and sour ingredients, is a time-honored Italian method of preserving vegetables, fish, and even meat. My first encounter with zucca in saor was at the agriturismo Ca' de Memi in Veneto, where chef Michela Tasca served deep-orange wedges of Mantovana squash topped with caramelized onions, raisins, and pine nuts, all drizzled with balsamic vinegar. It was a revelation, and now I re-create her recipe every autumn.

This dish is a versatile gem. Serve it as a side dish or as an appetizer to awaken your palate with its vibrant tangy-sweet notes.

Preheat the oven to 425°F/220°C with racks in the lower third and center positions. Line two baking sheets with parchment paper.

Peel the squash if the skin is very thick and remove the seeds. Cut the squash into wedges ¼ inch/6 mm thick, or half-moons, depending on the squash used. Cut the onions into rounds ¼ inch/6 mm thick.

In a small bowl, whisk together the olive oil and salt. Use a brush to coat the squash slices with the oil on both sides and arrange them in a single layer on one of the lined baking sheets. Repeat the process with the onions on the second pan. Make sure there's enough space between the pieces for them to roast properly; if they're crowded, they'll steam instead of caramelizing.

Transfer the baking sheets to the hot oven and roast the vegetables until tender and just starting to caramelize at the edges, 25 to 30 minutes, switching the positions of the racks halfway through. Set aside to cool.

Meanwhile, in a small saucepan, combine the white wine and 2 tablespoons of the balsamic vinegar and bring to a boil over medium heat. Add the raisins, reduce the heat, and simmer until they've plumped up, 3 to 5 minutes. Drain the raisins and place them on a paper towel to remove excess moisture.

On a large serving platter, arrange the roasted squash in one layer, drizzle with 1 tablespoon of the balsamic vinegar, then top with the roasted onions and drizzle with the remaining balsamic vinegar. Sprinkle with the pine nuts and the raisins, letting them nestle between the layers for little bursts of sweetness.

Let the dish sit at room temperature for at least 30 minutes before serving, allowing all the flavors to mingle and deepen.

Store leftovers in an airtight container in the fridge for up to 3 days. Bring to room temperature before serving for the best flavor.

LEFT: Extra-Nutty Lacinato Kale Salad
RIGHT: Sweet & Sour Squash

insalata russa

RUSSIAN SALAD

Serves 6 to 8 as a side dish

3 large eggs

FOR THE VEGETABLES

2 medium yellow waxy potatoes, peeled and diced

2 medium carrots, peeled and diced

2 medium zucchini, diced

1 cup/ 170 g frozen peas

Fine sea salt

FOR THE SALAD

14 cornichons, chopped (about ¼ cup/ 50 g)

20 Taggiasca or Kalamata olives, pitted and sliced into rounds

Fresh basil leaves

Fresh thyme sprigs, leaves picked

1 scant cup/ 200 g Vegan Mayonnaise (recipe follows)

Fine sea salt and freshly ground black pepper

Some trace the origins of this salad to Franco-Russian culinary exchanges during Napoleonic times, while others attribute it to Belgian-Russian chef Lucien Olivier, whose name the dish still bears in many countries. Yet another theory places its origin in nineteenth-century Piedmont, Italy. What we know for sure is that insalata russa was common and considered a delicate and elegant side dish in early-twentieth-century Italy, and nowadays it is a fixture of Neapolitan Christmas Eve tables.

While it's traditionally associated with festive winter celebrations, I make the salad during summer. Served chilled, straight from the fridge, it's a refreshing dish that helps beat the heat of the season. Serve insalata russa as a side dish alongside roasted or boiled fish or grilled white meats. For a satisfying summer meal, pair it with a simple tomato salad dressed with peppery olive oil and scattered with fresh basil leaves.

PREPARE THE EGGS: Bring a small pot of water to a rolling boil, then gently plunge the eggs into the water. Simmer the eggs for 10 minutes, then transfer them to a bowl of ice and water. This will make it easier to peel them. Peel the eggs and set them aside.

PREPARE THE VEGETABLES: As you cut up the potatoes, carrots, and zucchini, place them in separate bowls. Place the peas in another bowl.

Bring a large pot of water to a boil, then salt it generously. Adding one vegetable at a time (see Notes), cook the potatoes for 5 minutes, the carrots for about 5 minutes, the zucchini for 3 minutes, and the frozen peas for 5 minutes. Remove the vegetables with a slotted spoon, combine them in a colander, and pass them under cold water to stop the cooking. Let cool.

ASSEMBLE THE SALAD: Once all the vegetables are cooked and cooled, transfer them to a large bowl. Add the cornichons and sliced olives.

In a small bowl, mash 2 of the 3 hard-boiled eggs with a fork until crumbly, then add them to the vegetables. (Set aside the third egg to garnish the salad.) Add the basil, tearing up the leaves with your hands, and the thyme. Add the mayonnaise to the vegetables and mix gently and thoroughly. Taste and season with salt and pepper, if needed.

Arrange the insalata russa on a platter or a serving bowl, garnish with the remaining egg, cut into quarters, and refrigerate the salad for at least 1 hour before serving.

Store leftovers in an airtight container in the fridge for a day or two.

NOTES:

- By cutting the vegetables into the same size and cooking them separately, you will be able to cook them perfectly, avoiding mushy vegetables. The exact timing, though, will depend on the size of your vegetables and your taste. I prefer the vegetables to be cooked through but still al dente.
- To lighten the dish and add a tangy twist, replace half of the mayonnaise with Greek yogurt.
- While store-bought mayonnaise works, I prefer making a vegan version that's easy to whip up and inclusive for all guests. For an egg-like flavor, add a pinch of kala namak (Himalayan black salt), known for its sulfurous, egg-like aroma.
- Skip the hard-boiled eggs entirely if making the salad vegan.

VEGAN MAYONNAISE

Makes 2 scant cups/400 g

1 cup/240 ml cold-pressed sunflower oil

⅓ cup plus 1½ tablespoons/100 ml soy milk

2 tablespoons fresh lemon juice

2 tablespoons extra-virgin olive oil

1 tablespoon Dijon mustard

½ teaspoon fine sea salt

½ teaspoon ground turmeric

Pinch of kala namak (optional; see Notes)

Freshly ground black pepper

In the jug of an immersion blender (or in a stand blender), combine the sunflower oil, soy milk, lemon juice, olive oil, mustard, salt, turmeric, kala namak (if using), and a few turns of pepper. Blend for about 1 minute at high speed, until you get a thick mayonnaise. The mayonnaise will keep in an airtight container in the fridge for up to 4 days.

pasta fredda con peperoni arrostiti

ROASTED PEPPER PASTA SALAD

Serves 6 to 8 as a first course or light lunch

FOR THE ROASTED PEPPERS

4 bell peppers, 2 red and 2 yellow

¼ cup/60 ml extra-virgin olive oil

1½ teaspoons dried oregano

Fine sea salt and freshly ground black pepper

2 garlic cloves, smashed and peeled

FOR THE PASTA SALAD

Fine sea salt

1 pound/450 g short pasta, such as fusilli, cavatappi, farfalle, or more inventive shapes

1 cup/120 g Taggiasca or Kalamata olives, rinsed and pitted

¼ cup/20 g brined or salt-packed capers, thoroughly rinsed

2 handfuls of basil leaves, torn into pieces if big

Freshly ground black pepper

1 cup/100 g sliced almonds, lightly toasted

Extra-virgin olive oil (optional)

Pasta salads often suffer from a bad reputation, as most of the time they are coated in a ghastly mayonnaise. Not in Italy, though, where pasta salads are light, fresh, and generously dressed with extra-virgin olive oil.

From simple combinations like cherry tomatoes and basil to more elaborate creations featuring canned tuna, hard-boiled eggs, olives, capers, cheese, and pickled vegetables, pasta salads are a must in the summer. They can be a stand-alone main course on scorching days, a fuss-free weeknight dinner, or even a beachside meal packed in a cooler. They also make a perfect first course for an informal gathering.

ROAST THE PEPPERS: Preheat the oven to 450°F/230°C. Line a baking sheet with parchment paper.

Arrange the bell peppers on the lined baking sheet and transfer the pan to the oven. Roast the peppers, turning them frequently, until the skin is charred all over, about 40 minutes. If you want to further blacken the skin, pop them under the broiler for 5 more minutes.

Remove the peppers from the oven and, using tongs, carefully transfer them to a bowl. Be careful because they might contain steaming-hot liquid. Cover the bowl with plastic wrap and let the peppers cool down completely. The steam trapped in the bowl will make it easy to peel the peppers.

When the peppers are completely cool, peel and seed them, then cut each pepper into thin strips. Transfer the pepper strips to a colander and let the excess liquid drain off for about 30 minutes. This will avoid a watery dressing for the pasta salad.

Transfer the roasted peppers to a bowl and dress them with the olive oil, oregano, and salt and black pepper to taste. Add the smashed garlic to the bowl, stir, and cover with plastic wrap. (You can roast and dress the peppers up to 3 days ahead and store in an airtight container in the fridge.)

MAKE THE PASTA SALAD: Bring a large pot of water to a rolling boil and salt it generously. Add the pasta and cook until al dente according to the package directions. Drain the pasta and run it under cold water to stop the cooking.

-recipe continues-

NOTE: Cooking pasta for a salad requires a deliberate approach. Typically, when serving pasta hot, you would never rinse it, as this dilutes its taste. However, for pasta salads, rinsing is an essential extra step. Once cooked, drain the pasta and rinse it under cold running water; this prevents the pasta from overcooking from the residual heat and ensures a perfect texture when it's tossed with flavorful condiments.

Transfer the pasta to a large salad bowl and add the roasted peppers, olives, capers, and basil leaves. Use all the roasted pepper oil to dress the salad. Season with salt and pepper. Give the pasta salad a good stir, cover with plastic wrap, and stash in the fridge for a few hours before serving.

To serve, let the pasta salad mostly come back to room temperature, taste again to adjust the seasoning, add the toasted almonds, and refresh with a drizzle of extra-virgin olive oil if the salad looks a bit too dry.

Pasta salads are one of those dishes that keep on giving. Leftovers are great for 2 to 3 days if kept in an airtight container in the fridge.

panzanella autunnale

FALL PANZANELLA WITH SQUASH, CARROTS & FENNEL

Serves 8 as an appetizer; serves 4 to 6 as a main course

FOR THE ROASTED VEGETABLES

1 pound/450 g squash, such as Mantovana, kabocha, delicata, or butternut, peeled, seeded, and diced

3 carrots, peeled, halved lengthwise, and cut into half-moons

1 fennel bulb, outer layer removed, diced

¼ cup/60 ml extra-virgin olive oil

2 teaspoons fine sea salt

Freshly ground black pepper

Handful of fresh sage leaves

1 tablespoon apple cider vinegar

FOR THE QUICK PICKLED ONION

¼ cup/60 ml red wine vinegar

1 teaspoon fine sea salt

1 teaspoon sugar

1 small or ½ medium red onion, thinly sliced

-ingredients continue-

Simple and humble dishes that can be adapted to the changing seasons are a great resource to have in your cooking repertoire. Panzanella, a quintessentially Tuscan bread salad, is one of them. Typically made in the summer with tomatoes, cucumbers, fresh onions, and plenty of basil leaves, as the seasons shift, this classic can be reinterpreted with autumnal ingredients. This panzanella with squash, carrots, and fennel is a true celebration of fall flavors.

Serve as a seasonal appetizer, bringing the olive oil bottle to the table so that everyone can drizzle more as they please, or make a meal out of it, serving the salad with roasted sausages, pork chops, or a ball of creamy burrata.

ROAST THE VEGETABLES: Preheat the oven to 400°F/200°C.

Place the diced squash, carrots, and fennel on a baking sheet. Drizzle them with the olive oil and season with the salt and a few grinds of pepper. Add the sage leaves and apple cider vinegar; this will enhance all the flavors and prevent the vegetables from falling apart while baking. Toss until the vegetables are evenly coated. When they are all glistening with oil, spread them out on the baking sheet, ensuring they have enough space to caramelize rather than steam.

Transfer the vegetables to the hot oven and roast until soft and just starting to caramelize at the edges, 25 to 30 minutes. Set aside to cool. (The vegetables can be roasted a day ahead and kept in an airtight container in the fridge. Bring the vegetables to room temperature before making the salad.)

MEANWHILE, PREPARE THE PICKLED ONION: In a small saucepan, combine the red wine vinegar, ¼ cup/60 ml water, the salt, and sugar and warm over medium heat until the sugar has dissolved.

Turn off the heat, dump the red onion into the saucepan with the hot pickling liquid, and swirl the pot to make sure the onion is submerged. Let it rest at room temperature for 30 minutes.

-recipe continues-

FOR THE PANZANELLA

- 8 ounces/225 g stale Tuscan bread, sliced (about 2 thick slices from a crusty round boule)
- ½ cup/60 g Taggiasca or Kalamata olives, rinsed and pitted
- ¼ cup/20 g brined or salt-packed capers, thoroughly rinsed
- Leaves from a few fresh thyme sprigs
- Fine sea salt and freshly ground black pepper
- ¼ cup/60 ml olio nuovo, or your best extra-virgin olive oil, plus more to taste
- 2 tablespoons red wine vinegar

ASSEMBLE THE PANZANELLA: Break the stale bread into large chunks and place in a bowl. Cover with cold water and press down on the bread to fully submerge it. Let it soak for about 5 minutes, or until the bread has softened. Check it; it should have soaked up enough water to become soft again. If it's still a bit hard, let it soak a few minutes longer.

Drain the bread and, with your hands, squeeze out as much water as possible. When you think you have squeezed it enough, squeeze it again; a soggy panzanella is never enjoyable. Crumble the squeezed bread into a large bowl. It should resemble fluffy crumbs, almost like couscous.

Add the drained pickled onions, roasted vegetables, olives, capers, and thyme leaves to the bowl with the bread. Season with salt and pepper. Drizzle with the olive oil and red wine vinegar, then toss everything together until well combined. Taste and adjust the seasoning as needed.

Allow the panzanella to rest at room temperature for 30 minutes before serving, letting the flavors meld. Just before serving, add an extra drizzle of olive oil if the panzanella seems a bit dry.

Store leftovers in an airtight container in the fridge for up to 3 days. For the best flavor, bring the panzanella back to room temperature before serving.

NOTE: If there isn't a piece of stale bread in your kitchen to make the salad—a scenario nearly unthinkable in a Tuscan household—use these same vegetables to dress a hearty rice salad (see How to Make Insalata di Riso, page 228).

FRESH HERB PAIRINGS IN ITALIAN CUISINE

ITALIAN COOKING RELIES HEAVILY ON FRESH HERBS. You won't find dried herbs in our spice racks. Instead, we often pick them directly from a pot or the garden when the herbs are in season.

I am spoiled, as I've always had plenty of fresh herbs at my disposal in our garden. Throughout the year, sage bushes grow beneath the olive trees, and enormous rosemary plants line the fence. A bay tree shades the table where we sit in the afternoon for a chat. Wild fennel and calamint—a Mediterranean member of the mint family—appear spontaneously after the last frost, heralding the arrival of the good season. And in summer, basil and parsley take their turn in the garden.

Here are some of the most common herbs in Italian cuisine. Incorporating these fresh herbs into your recipes will instantly infuse your dishes with an Italian flair.

BASIL/BASILICO: Basil has the unmistakable scent of an Italian summer and is the star ingredient of Ligurian pesto, the most famous pesto in Italy. Add a few leaves of basil to a pan of sautéed zucchini, a tomato tonnato (see page 20), or a roasted pepper pasta salad (see page 33). A single leaf is always welcome in a jar of homemade tomato sauce (see page 221) or whole peeled tomatoes. We even rub basil leaves on our skin to ward off mosquito bites.

BAY LEAF/ALLORO: Add a fresh bay leaf to your meat sauces or whenever you're cooking beans, soups, and stews. It imparts a subtle woodsy aroma to preserves as well, such as baby artichokes in oil (see page 217), giardiniera (see page 226), or onion and apple jam (see page 234).

CALAMINT/NEPITELLA OR MENTUCCIA: Known as nepitella in Tuscany and mentuccia in Rome, calamint tastes like a mellow mint with fresh oregano undertones. It usually grows wild in fields, along cobblestone pathways, and in hedgerows. I never cook mushrooms or artichokes without it. You can grill porcini with a few sprigs of nepitella and a clove of garlic or make a pasta sauce with dried porcini and nepitella. Or add a few leaves to my sautéed or grilled eggplants. Use it generously with carciofi alla Romana (see page 43). If you can't find nepitella, try a combination of fresh oregano and mint instead.

MARJORAM/MAGGIORANA: An herb in the same family as oregano, marjoram is especially beloved and widely used in Ligurian cuisine for its mildly pungent, fresh, and herbaceous aroma. It pairs beautifully with eggs, mushrooms (as in porcini mushroom and ricotta stuffed crepes, see page 204), and sauces, imparting a delicate aroma to dishes like Ligurian-inspired potato-stuffed onions (see page 193).

MINT/MENTA: Mint is among the most versatile aromatic herbs in Italian cuisine. It is commonly used to season meats, grilled vegetables, desserts, and cocktails. When calamint isn't available, substitute mint for a similar flavor. For an unexpected twist, toss a handful of young mint leaves into your green salad; it will have the refreshing aroma of a garden in spring.

OREGANO/ORIGANO: This is perhaps the only herb we commonly use dried rather than fresh. It thrives along the coast, especially in southern Italy, and carries a distinct Mediterranean flavor. Pair it with tomatoes and peppers, use it in sun-dried tomatoes in oil (see page 229), or sprinkle it over mozzarella, pizza, potato and tomato salad (see page 23), or squash and eggplant pizzette capricciosa (see page 166).

PARSLEY/PREZZEMOLO: Parsley is such an underrated herb, often considered generic and lacking in personality. It's no wonder: Supermarket varieties are overgrown, with enormous, tough leaves that have already lost their fragrance. Young parsley is a completely different matter. Its tender leaves have a fresh, green, and woody taste. It especially complements briny ingredients, such as capers and olives, and most kinds of fish. I mostly use parsley with seafood and to make salsa verde (see page 153), the thick vinegary sauce made from plenty of parsley, capers, breadcrumbs, finely chopped hard-boiled eggs, and extra-virgin olive oil.

ROSEMARY/ROSMARINO: Rosemary grows in big bushes, a perennial ornament to Italian fields and gardens. Commonly used on roasted meat and fish, it also makes a perfect co-star for chickpeas, potatoes, and squash. Pair it with sage leaves and juniper berries to make a heady stock with woody undergrowth aromas for mushroom risotto (see page 117).

SAGE/SALVIA: Often associated with rosemary and garlic, sage is a perennial herb and a constant in many typical dishes throughout the year, from roasted potatoes to baked squash. Sage becomes a main character, though, when you fry it. Crisp the leaves in butter to dress stuffed pasta parcels like tortelli or roasted squash cappellacci (see page 199), or to use in olive oil to drizzle over boiled cannellini beans. Or dip them in batter first and deep-fry them until puffed and golden along with zucchini blossoms and other vegetables for an unforgettable appetizer (see page 130).

THYME/TIMO: Its strong, pungent aroma is somewhat reminiscent of rosemary. Use it when roasting or baking, as these methods best bring out thyme's fragrance. Try it in roasted carrots (see page 99), stuffed mushrooms (see page 196), or a summer vegetable gratin (see page 186).

WILD FENNEL/FINOCCHIETTO SELVATICO: It usually grows between spring and summer, when its feathery green fronds line country roads, alongside poppies, mint, and other wild herbs. In summer, the plants grow tall, topped with yellow umbrella-shaped flowers. Wild fennel is delicate and herbaceous, with a slight sweetness and a clean anise scent. Especially common in Sicilian and southern Italian cuisine, wild fennel fronds can be used with roasted fish or in a pesto with almonds and pecorino cheese, perfect for dressing fresh pasta or potato gnocchi.

BRAISED, BOILED & STEWED

Slow, gentle cooking methods coax out deep flavors and tender textures. From hearty soups to silky greens, these recipes highlight how time and patience transform humble vegetables into comforting dishes.

crostoni con carciofi alla Romana e mozzarella

ROMAN-STYLE ARTICHOKE & MOZZARELLA CROSTONI

Serves 8 as an appetizer

FOR THE ARTICHOKES

1 lemon

8 globe artichokes

3 tablespoons very finely chopped fresh flat-leaf parsley

3 tablespoons very finely chopped fresh mint or calamint

2 garlic cloves, minced

2 teaspoons fine sea salt

1 cup/240 ml extra-virgin olive oil

½ cup/120 ml dry white wine

FOR THE CROSTONI

8 slices country bread, about ¾ inch/2 cm thick

One 8-ounce/225 g ball fresh mozzarella, cut into bite-size pieces

8 anchovy fillets

In Rome, artichokes reign supreme in winter and spring. Local trattorias proudly feature two iconic dishes on their menus: carciofi alla giudia, where huge globe artichokes are double-fried until they bloom into golden, crisp flowers, and carciofi alla Romana, where the artichokes are gently braised in an aromatic bath of olive oil, white wine, garlic, and herbs. Slow-cooking transforms the artichokes into soft, silky, melt-in-your-mouth delicacies. While carciofi alla Romana shines when eaten on its own, the braise also makes a great topping for crostoni, paired with fresh mozzarella and anchovies, two other staples of Roman cuisine.

PREPARE THE ARTICHOKES: Grate the zest of ½ the lemon in a small bowl, then halve and squeeze the lemon into a large bowl of cold water. Add the two squeezed halves to the water.

Work with one artichoke at a time and transfer to the bowl of lemon water as you go. Remove the tough outer leaves, cut the prickly tip of the remaining leaves, then peel the base and stem with a paring knife, leaving about 1 inch/2.5 cm of stem attached to the base of each artichoke. Rub with a lemon half and plunge in the water. Tap the artichoke heads on a cutting board to loosen the leaves, then gently open them from the center, like a flower, and scoop out the fuzzy chokes with a small spoon.

Mix the lemon zest with the parsley, mint, garlic, salt, and 2 tablespoons of the olive oil, then fill each artichoke with the herb mixture.

Arrange the artichokes, stems up, in a pot where they can sit tightly next to each other. If there's too much space left in the pot to keep them in place, use the halved lemon you rubbed them with to prop them up. Pour in the remaining olive oil and the wine. Cover the pot with a double-folded piece of parchment paper, then place the lid on over the paper.

Cook the artichokes over low heat, with the cooking liquid bubbling around the artichokes, until they are dark green and soft and you can easily pierce the thickest part of the stem with a knife, 35 to 40 minutes.

-recipe continues-

NOTE: The artichokes can be kept in an airtight container in the fridge for about 5 days. Reheat them gently before making the crostoni.

Remove the artichokes from the pot with a slotted spoon (reserve the cooking liquid) and arrange them on a serving plate, stems up, then drizzle some of the reserved cooking liquid over the artichokes.

Serve at room temperature straightaway or use to make the crostoni.

MAKE THE CROSTONI: Preheat the oven to 400°F/200°C.

Quarter each artichoke and top the bread slices with artichokes and mozzarella bites. Nestle an anchovy fillet among the mozzarella bites so that it won't burn in the oven and will work as a surprise kick of flavor. Drizzle 1 teaspoon of the flavorful artichoke cooking liquid over each slice of bread.

Place the crostoni on a baking sheet, then transfer them to the hot oven and bake until the mozzarella starts to melt, about 8 minutes. Serve immediately.

HOW TO CLEAN AN ARTICHOKE

The following method for cleaning artichokes applies to both baby artichokes and regular-size ones.

- Halve a lemon and squeeze the juice into a bowl of water. This will prevent the artichokes from turning brown, as they oxidize quickly once cut. Rub the lemon on your hands, too. Keep the 2 lemon halves in the water to rub the artichokes as you work.
- Remove the tougher, darker outer leaves of each artichoke, pulling them downward and snapping them at the base. Be cruel and show no mercy; stop only when you reach the pale softer inner leaves. With a sharp knife, remove the spiky tips of the leaves, then pare the base and the stem, until you reach the whiter, softer interior.
- Rub the artichoke all over with a lemon half and plunge it into the bowl of acidulated water.

Friend
BBF

pasta e piselli

PEA & PASTA SOUP

Serves 4 as a first course

- 3 tablespoons extra-virgin olive oil
- ½ small yellow onion, finely minced (½ cup/80 g)
- 2 ounces/56 g guanciale or pancetta (optional), diced
- Fine sea salt
- 2 cups (10 ounces/280 g) peas, fresh or frozen
- About 4 cups/1 L hot water, lightly salted
- 6 ounces/170 g pasta mista, ditali, broken spaghetti, or other short dried pasta (about 1½ cups)
- 2 tablespoons grated Parmigiano Reggiano cheese
- 2 ounces/56 g provolone cheese, coarsely grated or cubed
- Freshly ground black pepper

NOTE: For a vegetarian version, skip the guanciale and add an extra tablespoon of olive oil.

In this comforting classic, pasta isn't boiled in a separate pot but is cooked directly in the saucepan with the stewed peas. This method, known in Italy as pasta risottata, involves adding water incrementally, much like adding stock to a risotto. With time, and a bit of stirring, the pasta releases its starches, melding beautifully with the pea cooking liquid to create a thick, creamy soup that clings to every spoonful.

Warm the olive oil in a medium saucepan over low heat. Add the onion, guanciale (if using), and a generous pinch of salt to prevent the onion from burning. Stir gently, allowing the onion to soften and the guanciale to release its flavor. Cook, stirring occasionally, until the onion is translucent and meltingly tender, about 10 minutes.

Stir in the peas, coating them in the oil until glossy and vibrant green. Pour in about 2 cups/500 ml of the lightly salted hot water, enough to just cover the peas, and bring the soup to a gentle simmer. Cover the saucepan and cook, stirring occasionally, until the peas begin to soften, about 5 minutes.

Pour the pasta directly into the saucepan, followed by an additional 1 cup/240 ml of lightly salted hot water and stir thoroughly. Continue cooking at a gentle simmer over medium-low heat, adding the remaining water incrementally as the pasta absorbs the liquid. Stir frequently to ensure even cooking and prevent sticking. This gradual process takes 15 to 20 minutes.

When the pasta is cooked through and the soup has a lusciously thick, creamy texture, remove the saucepan from the heat. Stir in the grated Parmigiano and provolone, mixing energetically until the cheeses melt into the soup.

Taste the soup and adjust the seasoning with salt and a few generous turns of pepper. Ladle the soup into warm bowls and serve immediately.

Any leftover soup can be stored in an airtight container in the fridge for up to 2 days. Reheat gently over low heat, adding a splash of hot water to restore the soup's creamy texture if needed.

peperonata

SWEET & SOUR PEPPER STEW

Serves 6 to 8 as a side dish

1/3 cup/80 ml extra-virgin olive oil

2 small red onions (about 5 ounces/140 g each), thinly sliced

2 teaspoons fine sea salt, plus more to taste

4 bell peppers, red and yellow (about 2¼ pounds/1 kg total)

1 tablespoon tomato paste

One 14-ounce/400 g can whole peeled tomatoes, crushed

3 tablespoons red wine vinegar, plus more to taste

1 teaspoon sugar (optional; see Notes)

10 fresh basil leaves, torn

NOTES:

- Choose a sturdy, wide pan to allow the peppers enough space to stew evenly, which helps them cook more quickly. If they are crammed into a small pot, the cooking may be uneven.
- When tomatoes are in season, fresh ripe ones can be used instead of canned peeled tomatoes for a brighter flavor.
- Sugar is optional; taste the raw peppers first, and if they are naturally sweet and fruity, you can skip adding it.

August and September are the peak months for sweet bell peppers, when their flavor is at its most vibrant and enticing. This is when I make peperonata, a southern Italian sweet-and-sour pepper stew. To prepare peperonata, red and yellow bell peppers are stewed with onions, tomatoes, and plenty of extra-virgin olive oil until meltingly soft. A few tablespoons of red wine vinegar add a sharp, refreshing note that brightens the dish.

Peperonata leftovers can keep on giving for many meals, as its flavors deepen overnight. Like many Italian stews, it's actually better the next day. Serve it warm or at room temperature as a side to roast chicken, a grilled pork chop, or a fried egg. It's also wonderful as a bruschetta topping, especially with a few pieces of creamy burrata.

Cover the bottom of a large saucepan with the extra-virgin olive oil, then add the onions and sprinkle with 1 teaspoon of the salt. The salt will help the onions sweat gently in the olive oil. Cook the onions over medium-low heat until soft and translucent, 12 to 15 minutes. Take care not to burn them, or they'll give a bitter taste to the peperonata.

Meanwhile, cut the peppers lengthwise into quarters and discard the seeds, stems, and any pithy white bits. Cut them into strips about ⅜ inch/8 mm wide.

When the onions are soft, stir in the tomato paste and cook for a couple of minutes over medium heat to caramelize it and develop its flavor. Add the peppers and the remaining 1 teaspoon salt and cook over medium-high heat, stirring often, until glistening with oil and slightly softened, about 15 minutes.

Add the crushed tomatoes, vinegar, and sugar (if using). Stir well, cover, and cook over medium-low heat until the peppers are meltingly soft and everything comes together into a thick stew, about 45 minutes. It might take up to 1 hour if your peppers are a bit tough; check them and taste them.

Taste and adjust the seasoning, should it need more salt. If you want a brighter taste, add a dash more vinegar to sharpen it up. Add the torn basil leaves, stir, and set aside so the stew can rest for a couple of hours before serving.

Leftover peperonata can be kept in an airtight container in the fridge for up to 3 days. Serve at room temperature or warm it gently over low heat.

fagiolini in umido

STEWED GREEN BEANS

Serves 6 to 8 as a side dish

- 2 pounds/900 g green beans
- ½ cup/120 ml extra-virgin olive oil
- 1 medium red onion, thinly sliced
- 6 Roma (plum) tomatoes, chopped
- Fine sea salt
- 1 cup/240 ml warm water
- Handful of fresh basil leaves, bigger leaves torn

Italians are known for their slow-cooked vegetables, which can often verge on being overcooked for an unsuspecting palate. When in the kitchen, overcooking vegetables requires a leap of faith, especially if you are used to al dente vegetables. So please trust me with this recipe and cook these green beans for more than an hour, on the lowest heat, with onions and tomatoes. Control your urge to turn off the heat when the beans are still crisp and grant them a long, transformative cooking. You want them buttery soft. Serve them as a side dish accompanied by a piece of crusty bread to mop up the juices.

Rinse the green beans thoroughly and drain in a colander. You don't need to cut both ends of the green beans. It's enough to trim just the stem end. Snap it off with your fingers and gently pull it downward to remove the string that runs along the length of the green bean.

Green beans will shrink when cooked for a long time. Choose a large pot that can accommodate all the green beans, and make sure it has a tight-fitting heavy lid. Pour the olive oil on the bottom and add the finely sliced onion and chopped tomatoes. Season with a generous pinch of salt. Pile the green beans on top and cover the pot with the lid.

Place the pot over medium heat and cook until you start to smell the sautéed onions, about 8 minutes.

Uncover, season with salt, and add the warm water. Cover again, reduce the heat to medium-low, and cook, stirring occasionally, until the beans are buttery soft, slightly wrinkled, and dark green, with a reddish, flavorful cooking liquid clinging to them, about 1 hour 20 minutes. If the pan becomes too dry, add a ladle of warm water. Taste and adjust the seasoning if needed, then add the basil leaves and let it sit at room temperature for a few minutes, so the leaves can release their aroma.

Keep leftovers in an airtight container in the fridge for 3 to 4 days. Reheat thoroughly before serving.

VARIATION:

Stewed Tuscan Green Beans

Finely mince 1 celery stalk, 1 carrot, and 1 red onion and use them in place of the sliced onion. Add 3½ ounces/100 g pancetta, cut into strips, and 2 chopped Roma (plum) tomatoes. Cook as in the recipe until the beans are buttery soft.

zuppa frantoiana

BEAN, LACINATO KALE & SQUASH SOUP

Makes 12 cups; serves 8 to 12

FOR THE BORLOTTI BEANS

8 ounces/225 g dried borlotti beans (see Notes) or cranberry beans (about 1¼ cups)

2 fresh sage leaves

1 bay leaf

1 garlic clove, smashed and peeled

A few black peppercorns

Fine sea salt

FOR THE SOUP

¼ cup/60 ml extra-virgin olive oil, plus more for drizzling

½ yellow onion, finely chopped

1 teaspoon fennel seeds, finely crushed

Fine sea salt

2 carrots, peeled, halved lengthwise, and sliced

2 medium yellow potatoes (about 1 pound/450 g total), diced

1 pound/450 g pumpkin or any winter squash, peeled, seeded, and diced

7 ounces/200 g lacinato kale (about a medium bunch), tough stems and midribs removed and discarded, leaves sliced into ribbons

-ingredients continue-

Zuppa frantoiana is named for *frantoio*, which means "olive oil mill," as the soup was traditionally prepared during the olive harvest season in Tuscany. This hearty broth celebrates simple ingredients like beans, leafy greens, and stale bread, all elevated by a generous drizzle of olio nuovo, the peppery, vibrant freshly pressed extra-virgin olive oil.

If you're lucky enough to get your hands on a precious bottle of new olive oil, don't hesitate to use it generously to finish your soup as well.

COOK THE BEANS: Place the dried borlotti beans in a large bowl and cover them with plenty of cold water, ensuring the water is several inches above the beans. Let them soak at room temperature for at least 12 hours, or overnight.

Drain and rinse the soaked beans thoroughly, then transfer them to a large pot. Choose a pot with enough space for the beans to double in volume as they cook. Fill the pot two-thirds full with water, ensuring the beans are completely submerged. Add the sage leaves, bay leaf, garlic, and peppercorns.

Bring the water to a gentle simmer over medium-low heat. Once it starts simmering, reduce the heat to low, cover the pot, and cook the beans until they are tender, with a buttery texture and thin, translucent skins. Depending on the size and age of the beans, this process may take a couple of hours. Keep an eye on the water level, adding more hot water as needed to ensure the beans remain submerged.

When the beans are tender, season generously with salt. Let the beans rest in their liquid until ready to use.

MAKE THE SOUP: Scoop out roughly half of the cooked beans from the pot with a slotted spoon, transfer them to a bowl, and set them aside. Discard the sage leaves, bay leaf, and garlic. Using an immersion blender, puree the remaining beans with all their cooking liquid to make a smooth, brownish stock. Set aside.

In a large pot, heat the olive oil over low heat. Add the onion, fennel seeds, and a generous pinch of salt to prevent the onion from burning. Cook, stirring frequently, until the onion is soft and translucent, about 10 minutes.

-recipe continues-

8 ounces/225 g Swiss chard (about a medium bunch), tough stems removed and discarded, leaves sliced into ribbons

Freshly ground black pepper

8 to 12 slices day-old crusty bread, toasted

Pour in the pureed beans, cover, increase the heat to medium, and bring to a boil. Add the carrots, potatoes, squash, and kale, then season with 1 teaspoon salt. Reduce the heat to maintain a vigorous simmer and cook uncovered for about 30 minutes, stirring occasionally.

Stir in the reserved whole beans and the Swiss chard. Reduce the heat to low and cook, covered, stirring often to prevent sticking, until the soup is creamy and thick, and the vegetables are meltingly soft, about 1½ hours. Taste and adjust the seasoning with additional salt and pepper as needed.

Place a toasted slice of bread at the bottom of each serving bowl and drizzle it with olive oil. Ladle the soup over the bread and finish with an extra drizzle of olive oil.

This soup is even better the next day. Let it cool completely, then cover and refrigerate. Reheat gently over low heat, adding a bit of water if necessary to adjust the consistency.

NOTES:

- You can cook the borlotti beans in advance and store them in their cooking liquid in the fridge for up to 3 days. To keep them longer, drain the cooking liquid and freeze the beans and liquid separately for your soup.
- If you prefer a shortcut, use two 15-ounce/425 g cans of good-quality canned beans. Rinse them thoroughly before using and use 6½ cups/1.5 L warm water in the soup in place of the bean cooking liquid.

vellutata di patate e verza con crostini alla senape e Parmigiano

SAVOY CABBAGE & POTATO SOUP WITH MUSTARD & CHEESY CROUTONS

Serves 4 to 6

FOR THE SOUP

¼ cup/60 ml extra-virgin olive oil

1 shallot, thinly sliced

1 leek, white and light green parts only, thinly sliced

6 fresh sage leaves

1 bay leaf

Fine sea salt

2 starchy potatoes, such as russets, peeled and diced (about 1 pound/450 g total)

½ small head Savoy or green cabbage (about 12 ounces/350 g), finely sliced, outer leaves removed (see Note)

1 celery stalk, thinly sliced

Freshly ground black pepper

FOR THE CHEESY CROUTONS

4 tablespoons extra-virgin olive oil

1 tablespoon Dijon mustard

4 slices crusty bread (about 5 ounces/150 g total), cubed

6 fresh sage leaves

1 garlic clove, unpeeled

1 ounce/28 g Parmigiano Reggiano cheese, finely grated (about ⅓ cup firmly packed)

-ingredients continue-

At first glance, this ingredients list seems like a collection of vegetables that often linger in the fridge or pantry waiting for a purpose. But with a bit of slow cooking, half a head of cabbage, a few potatoes, a shallot, a leek, and a stalk of celery melt into a creamy, comforting soup that feels like a warm embrace on a chilly day.

A topping of cheesy croutons, enriched with the bold flavors of garlic, sage, mustard, and Parmigiano Reggiano cheese, adds a savory crunch that beautifully contrasts the sturdy and reliable cabbage and potato soup.

MAKE THE SOUP: Cover the bottom of a medium pot with the olive oil. Add the shallot, leek, sage leaves, and bay leaf and season with a big pinch of salt. Cook over low heat, stirring occasionally, until soft and translucent, about 15 minutes.

Add the potatoes, cabbage, and celery and season with salt. Stir and cook over low heat for about 5 minutes to allow the flavors to meld.

Pour in enough hot water to cover the vegetables. Cover and cook over medium heat, stirring occasionally, until soft, about 30 minutes. You should be able to easily mash the potatoes with a wooden spoon against the sides of the pot.

MEANWHILE, MAKE THE CHEESY CROUTONS: In a medium bowl, mix 3 tablespoons of the olive oil and the mustard. Toss the bread cubes in the seasoning until evenly coated.

In a medium skillet, warm the remaining 1 tablespoon olive oil over medium heat. Add the sage leaves and garlic clove and cook until the sage is crisp and the garlic is golden and has released its aroma into the oil. Discard the garlic, then add the bread cubes, shaking the pan to distribute them evenly. Fry, stirring often and scraping the bottom of the pan, until the croutons are golden brown and toasted, 5 to 7 minutes.

Sprinkle the grated Parmigiano over the croutons, tossing them quickly in the pan until the cheese melts and coats each piece, about 2 minutes. Remove from the heat and set aside.

-recipe continues-

FOR SERVING

Extra-virgin olive oil, for drizzling

Freshly ground black pepper

Discard the sage and bay leaf from the soup and blend all the vegetables with an immersion blender until smooth. (Alternatively, carefully blend in a stand blender, working in batches as needed, and return to the pot.) Taste and adjust the seasoning with salt and pepper. Simmer the soup over medium heat for about 10 minutes, or until it reaches the thickness you like.

TO SERVE: Ladle the soup into serving bowls. Drizzle with a bit of olive oil, add a sprinkle of pepper, and top generously with the cheesy croutons.

Any leftover soup can be kept in an airtight container in the fridge for up to 3 days, while leftover croutons can be kept in an airtight container at room temperature. To reheat, warm the soup gently over low heat until heated through, stirring occasionally to maintain its creamy texture.

NOTE: Save the tougher outer leaves to make the Stuffed Cabbage Rolls (page 211).

cavolfiore soffocato

SMOTHERED CAULIFLOWER WITH OLIVES & SUN-DRIED TOMATOES

Serves 4 as a side dish

1 medium cauliflower (about 2¼ pounds/1 kg)

¼ cup/60 ml extra-virgin olive oil

2 garlic cloves, unpeeled

⅔ cup/90 g Taggiasca or Kalamata olives, pitted

1 cup/50 g oil-packed sun-dried tomatoes, chopped

Fine sea salt

My husband, Tommaso, didn't care much for cauliflower until he tasted cavolfiore soffocato, a Sardinian dish that completely transforms this humble vegetable. The florets are first browned in olive oil, which brings out their natural nuttiness, then gently stewed with a splash of water until they are smothered in the steam—hence the name—becoming soft and sweet. To finish, olives and sun-dried tomatoes are added, elevating the dish with bursts of umami and saltiness.

Serve this as a side for roast chicken or pork chops or enjoy it with crusty bread and aged pecorino cheese for a satisfying rustic meal.

Break the cauliflower into small florets and transfer to a colander. Add also a few small, tender cauliflower leaves. Rinse thoroughly under running water, then set aside to drain.

Pour the olive oil into a medium skillet, add the unpeeled garlic cloves, and cook them gently over medium heat for about 5 minutes, until you can smell the garlic aroma.

Without drying the florets, carefully add them to the skillet: Watch out for any oil splatters! Cook over medium heat, stirring often with a wooden spoon, until the florets begin to take on some color, turning golden in spots, about 10 minutes.

Pour ¼ cup/60 ml water into the skillet, cover, reduce the heat to medium-low, and cook the cauliflower until you can easily pierce it with the tip of a knife, about 30 minutes, checking it occasionally. The cauliflower will smother in the steam, becoming tender and preserving all its flavor.

Stir in the olives and sun-dried tomatoes and cook for 5 more minutes, allowing all the flavors to mingle. Taste and adjust the seasoning with salt.

Serve the cauliflower immediately or refrigerate in an airtight container for up to 3 days. Reheat it gently in the microwave, or in a pan with a few drops of olive oil, before serving.

Tre - C.
millennium

friggione

ONION & TOMATO STEW

Makes about 2 cups; serves 4 to 6 as an appetizer

- 2 pounds/900 g yellow onions
- 1 teaspoon sugar
- Fine sea salt
- 2 tablespoons extra-virgin olive oil
- 1 tablespoon tomato paste
- 4 ounces/115 g canned peeled tomatoes, crushed (passata or canned crushed tomatoes also work)
- Chili oil (optional; see Note)
- Grilled polenta or toasted bread, for serving

Friggione, a traditional Bolognese onion spread, is a dish that invites abundance—it's perfect for making in large quantities, whether for a cozy family dinner or a lively gathering. Traditionally served with boiled meats or tigelle—thin, round breads from the Apennine Mountains, usually eaten with cold cuts—friggione is wonderfully versatile. It's delicious as a topping for crostini or polenta, or as a sauce for pasta. And leftovers can spark creativity: Our friend Neri cooks friggione with flaked steamed cod, transforming it into a spectacular dressing for rigatoni.

Thinly slice the onions. A mandoline will make this step quicker and save you some tears. Place the sliced onions in a large pot, sprinkle with the sugar and 1 teaspoon salt, and toss to coat evenly. Cover the pot with a lid and let the onions macerate at room temperature for about 2 hours. During this time, they will release their natural juices, enhancing their sweetness.

Add the olive oil to the pot and place it over low heat. Cover and cook the onions, stirring occasionally to prevent sticking. Let them gently cook until they are golden, creamy, and reduced to one-third of their original volume—this can take up to 3 hours, but the result is worth the wait.

Now build the flavor. Stir in the tomato paste and let it caramelize for 2 minutes over medium heat, releasing its rich umami depth. Add the crushed tomatoes and stir. Reduce the heat to the lowest setting, cover, and cook, stirring frequently, until the mixture becomes glossy, creamy, and deeply flavorful, about 45 minutes.

Generously season the friggione with salt to balance the onions' natural sweetness. For a hint of heat, drizzle in a few drops of chili oil.

Serve hot or warm in winter, or cold during summer, paired with grilled polenta or toasted bread.

Friggione keeps well in the fridge for up to 5 days when stored in an airtight container. To enjoy it warm, gently reheat over low heat or in the microwave.

NOTE: Though not traditional, finish friggione with a few drops of chili oil for an extra kick.

TWICE-COOKED

Italian cuisine often relies on double-cooking techniques—first boiling a vegetable, then sautéing or roasting it—to layer textures and flavors. This approach softens fibrous vegetables before crisping their edges or blending them into creamy fillings.

---

spaghetti aglio, olio e agretti

AGLIO & OLIO SPAGHETTI WITH MONK'S BEARD

Serves 4

- Fine sea salt
- 10 ounces/300 g agretti (see Notes), about 1 bunch
- ¼ cup/60 ml extra-virgin olive oil
- 2 garlic cloves, minced
- Red pepper flakes
- 14 ounces/400 g spaghetti
- 2 to 3 tablespoons grated mullet bottarga (optional; see Notes)

NOTES:

- If you can't find agretti, try this recipe with the same amount (about 10 ounces/300 g) of dandelion greens. Trim the stems and cut the leaves into thin ribbons. Blanch them for just 1 minute to avoid overcooking.
- Bottarga, a beloved and traditional Italian ingredient, is the salted roe of tuna or mullet. With its distinctive briny taste, it brings depth, saltiness, and an umami-rich complexity to any dish. If bottarga is difficult to find, a generous sprinkling of grated pecorino can offer a similar savory kick.

The scientific name for agretti is *Salsola soda*, but they are known in Italy as *barba di frate* or "monk's beard." Agretti grow in sandy seashores along the Mediterranean coast and are especially popular in Tuscany. Agretti goes well with pasta and seafood. The leaves of agretti look like chives, and they have a succulent texture that has a nice crunch when eaten raw. Cleaning the agretti is a form of meditation: You must rinse them in plenty of water and remove all the pinkish roots. One by one. Buy more than you would think is enough; they shrink in the pan once cooked.

Bring a large pot of water to a rolling boil and salt it lightly (agretti have a savory taste on their own).

While the water heats, clean the agretti. Fill your sink with water and rinse the agretti by shaking them in the water. Then, one by one, remove their pinkish roots and transfer the cleaned agretti to a colander. Rinse them once more.

Prepare a bowl with icy cold water and set near the stove. Plunge the agretti into the boiling water. Submerge them with a spoon and blanch for 3 minutes, then drain the agretti and drop them into the ice water.

Bring another large pot of water to a rolling boil and salt it generously.

While the water heats, in a large skillet, heat the olive oil over medium-low heat. Add the garlic and pepper flakes—just enough for a gentle warmth that won't overpower the delicate flavors. Cook the garlic for 3 to 5 minutes, stirring often, so it infuses the oil without browning. The garlic should soften but remain pale (browning will turn it bitter).

Drain the agretti and toss them in the garlicky oil over medium heat for about 2 minutes, until glistening and coated with oil.

Cook the spaghetti in the boiling water until al dente according to the package directions.

Reserving about 1 cup/240 ml of the pasta water, drain the spaghetti and add it to the pan with the agretti, tossing everything together over medium heat, about 3 minutes, to weave the agretti strands with the pasta. If it looks too dry, add some of the reserved pasta water, tossing energetically to create a silky, creamy sauce.

Remove from the heat and scatter the grated bottarga (if using) on top. Serve immediately.

RAFFO
GREZZA

polpette di melanzane

EGGPLANT CROQUETTES

Makes 14 to 16 croquettes

- 2 medium eggplants (about 1½ pounds/680 g total)
- 7 ounces/200 g day-old rustic or country-style bread (2 to 3 thick slices), crusts removed, plus more if needed
- 3½ ounces/100 g Parmigiano Reggiano cheese, finely grated (about 1¾ cups firmly packed)
- 3½ ounces/100 g sliced prosciutto cotto or cooked ham, cut into thin strips
- 1 garlic clove, finely minced
- 1 tablespoon finely chopped fresh parsley
- 1 tablespoon finely chopped fresh basil
- Fine sea salt and freshly ground black pepper
- 1 large egg, lightly beaten
- ½ cup/63 g all-purpose flour, plus a bit more
- 4¼ cups/1 L vegetable oil, such as sunflower or peanut, for frying

When a new bakery opened in my town, I gained an incredible source for artisanal sourdough bread *and* a kindred spirit in Maria Rosa, the baker behind Forno Pellegrino. I introduced Maria Rosa to our local way of upcycling stale bread, while she shared her secrets for turning seasonal vegetables into some of Calabria's most iconic dishes, like these croquettes.

In Calabrian summer cuisine, eggplants reign supreme—fried, grilled, stewed, or preserved for the colder months. In the heat of summer, eggplants are boiled until silky, then combined with bread, herbs, cheese, and prosciutto to create little bombs of flavor. These croquettes are delicious hot and freshly fried but are just as satisfying served at room temperature as part of a summer appetizer spread.

Bring a large pot of water to a boil. Rinse the eggplants and cut them into about 2-inch/5 cm chunks, then add them to the boiling water and boil until translucent and you can easily pierce them with a knife, 5 to 8 minutes. Drain the eggplants and let them cool in a colander.

While the eggplants are cooling, crumble the bread by rubbing it between your palms: You should obtain soft, feathery, fine crumbs.

When the eggplants are cool enough to handle, squeeze as much water as possible from the flesh. Don't worry if they break up; you're going to mash them anyway. Transfer the squeezed eggplants—pulp and skin—to a bowl. Add the grated Parmigiano Reggiano cheese, prosciutto cotto, minced garlic, chopped parsley, and basil. Use your hands and mix thoroughly to combine, then season to taste with salt and pepper. Stir in the beaten egg. The filling should be thick and dense, not watery at all.

Pour the ½ cup/63 g flour onto a large plate and place another plate nearby, lightly dusted with flour.

To form the eggplant croquettes, scoop ¼ cup/60 g of the mixture. With slightly wet hands, roll into a ball, gently shape the ball into an oval-shaped croquette, and flatten it lightly. Roll it in the flour to coat and place it on the lightly floured plate. Repeat with the remaining filling.

-recipe continues-

Line a baking sheet with parchment paper and have near the stove. In a large, deep pot, heat the oil over medium-high heat to 350°F/175°C on a deep-frying thermometer, or until the handle of a wooden spoon dipped in the oil is immediately surrounded by tiny bubbles.

Working in two batches to avoid overcrowding, fry the eggplant croquettes until golden brown, about 8 minutes, flipping them from time to time. Transfer them with a slotted spoon to the lined baking sheet. Make sure the oil returns to temperature between batches.

Serve the croquettes hot or at room temperature.

Leftover eggplant croquettes can be kept in the fridge for a couple of days. Reheat them gently in a hot oven or the microwave before serving.

carciofi e patate

DOUBLE-COOKED ARTICHOKES & POTATOES

Serves 4 as a small side dish

FOR THE SALMORIGLIO

½ cup/ 120 ml extra-virgin olive oil

¼ cup/60 ml fresh lemon juice

2 garlic cloves, smashed and peeled

2 teaspoons dried oregano

1 teaspoon dried mint

1 teaspoon fine sea salt

Grated zest of ½ lemon

Red pepper flakes

FOR THE ARTICHOKES AND POTATOES

1 lemon

4 artichokes

1 garlic clove, unpeeled

1 carrot

1 celery stalk

½ yellow onion, unpeeled

1 sprig parsley

2 tablespoons coarse sea salt

½ teaspoon black peppercorns

1 pound/450 g yellow waxy potatoes (3 to 4 small), peeled and cut into 1-inch/2.5 cm chunks

FOR SERVING

1 tablespoon chopped fresh mint

1 tablespoon chopped fresh parsley

Double-cooking is a surefire way to elevate the texture of boiled vegetables. In this recipe, inspired by a dish served at Via Carota in New York City, tender artichokes and potatoes, gently simmered in an aromatic stock, are transformed with a final sear in a hot pan drenched in salmoriglio, a tangy blend of olive oil, lemon, garlic, and herbs. The result is a dish where the vegetables have soft, mellow interiors and irresistibly crisp, golden exteriors.

Serve it as a side with lamb chops or roast chicken or top with some crumbled goat cheese to turn it into a main course.

MAKE THE SALMORIGLIO: In a small bowl, whisk together the olive oil, lemon juice, smashed garlic, oregano, mint, fine salt, lemon zest, and pepper flakes to taste. Set the mixture aside at room temperature for about 1 hour to let the flavors infuse, then remove and discard the garlic. The salmoriglio can be prepared in advance and stored in the fridge for up to 5 days. Remove it from the fridge, bring it back to room temperature, and whisk well before using.

PREPARE THE ARTICHOKES AND POTATOES: Peel the lemon zest off the lemon with a peeler and collect the strips in a small bowl. Halve and squeeze the lemon into a large bowl of cold water. Add the two squeezed halves to the water.

To prepare the artichokes, remove the tough outer leaves, cut the prickly tips of the inner leaves, then pare the bases and stems of the artichokes, leaving about 1 inch/2.5 cm of stem attached to the base of each artichoke. Rub them with a lemon half, cut them in half, and scoop out the fuzzy chokes. Submerge the halved artichokes in the acidulated water. Set aside.

Meanwhile, line a baking sheet with a clean kitchen towel and set near the stove. Fill a large pot with water, then add the reserved lemon zest strips, garlic clove, carrot, celery, onion, parsley sprig, coarse salt, and peppercorns. Add the potatoes, cover, and bring to a boil over high heat. Reduce the heat and simmer until the potatoes can be easily pierced with a knife, 20 to 25 minutes.

-recipe continues-

When the potatoes are ready, remove them from the pot with a slotted spoon and transfer them to one side of the lined baking sheet. Discard the vegetables and aromatics.

Bring the cooking liquid back to a boil, then plunge the artichokes into the pot. Submerge them with a slotted spoon and cook over medium heat, covered, until you can easily pierce them with a knife. If the artichokes are smaller than an apricot, cook them for about 10 minutes; otherwise, if they are the size of big lemons, cook them for up to 20 minutes. The artichokes should retain some bite.

Drain the artichokes and arrange them cut side down on the empty half of the lined baking sheet so that they can drain any excess moisture. Once drained, you can store the artichokes and potatoes in the fridge in an airtight container for a couple of days or continue with the recipe.

Lift the towel of vegetables off the sheet pan, then carefully spill them back onto the towel-free pan. Brush them with salmoriglio, reserving about ¼ cup for serving.

Warm a large nonstick skillet over medium-high heat. Cook the artichokes cut side down for about 3 minutes, until golden brown and nicely charred, then flip them and cook them for 3 more minutes. Transfer the artichokes to a serving platter.

Cook the potatoes, about 4 minutes per side, until golden brown, then arrange them on the serving dish with the artichokes.

TO SERVE: Drizzle the artichokes and potatoes with the remaining salmoriglio, if desired, sprinkle with chopped fresh mint and parsley, and serve immediately.

Keep any leftovers in the fridge for a couple of days and reheat thoroughly in a hot pan before serving. If you have leftover salmoriglio, keep it in an airtight container in the fridge for up to 5 days. It can be drizzled over the reheated leftovers to add a fresh kick.

NOTE: If fresh artichokes are unavailable, substitute with 6 ounces/ 170 g frozen artichoke quarters. Thaw them overnight in the fridge and they'll be ready to use.

pizza di scarola

ESCAROLE PIE

Serves 6 to 8

FOR THE DOUGH

1 small starchy potato, such as russet (about 5 ounces/ 150 g)

1⅔ cups/ 200 g all-purpose flour, plus more for dusting

1 cup plus 2 tablespoons/ 200 g semolina flour

½ teaspoon active dry yeast

½ teaspoon sugar

1 teaspoon fine sea salt

2 tablespoons extra-virgin olive oil, plus more for greasing

FOR THE FILLING

3 pounds/ 1.4 kg escarole (2 to 3 heads)

Fine sea salt

⅓ cup/ 80 ml extra-virgin olive oil, plus more for drizzling

4 oil-packed anchovy fillets, chopped

2 garlic cloves, smashed and peeled

Red pepper flakes

3 tablespoons pitted Gaeta or Kalamata olives

2 tablespoons brined or salt-packed capers, rinsed

2 tablespoons pine nuts, toasted

Despite the name, this is not a traditional pizza. Instead, it's a stuffed focaccia or savory pie belonging to the Neapolitan tradition, with a soft crust made with potato bread dough. Escarole is the protagonist, its bitterness tamed by supporting Mediterranean flavors: pine nuts, black olives, capers, and anchovies, along with the ubiquitous extra-virgin olive oil and red pepper flakes.

In Naples, escarole pie is usually served as a hearty side dish or appetizer for Christmas Eve and New Year's Eve, when meat is banned from the festive menus. I love to make this escarole pie throughout winter whenever I have friends over for dinner and I want something that just needs to be sliced. Leftovers are great in your lunchbox the next day.

MAKE THE DOUGH: Peel the potato, cube it, and place it in a small pot. Fill the pot with cold water, bring to a boil over high heat, then reduce to a simmer and cook the potato until you can easily mash it with a wooden spoon against the edges of the pot. Reserving the cooking liquid for the dough, drain the potato.

Transfer the potato to a plate and mash immediately with a fork. It's easier to do this when the potato is still steaming hot to avoid lumps in the dough. Set the mashed potato aside to cool.

Wait until the mashed potato and its water have cooled to lukewarm before making the bread, as the heat will kill the yeast and result in a heavy dough for your pie.

In a bowl, combine the all-purpose flour, semolina flour, mashed potato, yeast, sugar, and ¾ cup/180 ml of the potato cooking liquid and knead by hand, squeezing the dough between your fingers, until you have incorporated all the flour and have a rough dough ball. In the beginning, the dough will be sticky, then it will get smoother and silkier.

Add the salt and another tablespoon of the potato cooking liquid, transfer to a wooden board, and keep kneading, pushing, and stretching for at least 10 minutes, until the dough is elastic, slightly moist, and smooth.

Add the olive oil and knead briefly until fully absorbed. You may need to squeeze the dough to help the oil penetrate. (Alternatively, knead in a stand mixer with the dough hook for about 10 minutes on low speed, then finish kneading by hand for 5 minutes.)

Roll the dough into a ball, transfer to a lightly greased bowl, cover with a damp kitchen towel, and let it rest at room temperature until it doubles in size, about 2 hours.

NOTE: If you want to skip the dough, the filling is also delicious on its own. Serve it as a side dish to grilled pork chops, or atop a slice of garlic-rubbed toast, crowned with a soft-boiled egg.

MEANWHILE, MAKE THE FILLING: Rinse the escarole under running water and separate the leaves. Bring a large pot of water to a rolling boil and salt it generously. Blanch the escarole in two batches: Submerge the escarole with a spoon and cook just until the water starts boiling again, then remove them with kitchen tongs and transfer to a colander. Repeat and cook the remaining escarole.

Drain the escarole and let it cool down until you can easily handle it. Working in batches, squeeze the escarole into small balls to remove excess water. Roughly chop and set aside.

Pour the olive oil into a large saucepan and add the anchovies, garlic, and pepper flakes to taste. Warm over low heat for about 5 minutes, stirring to dissolve the anchovies.

When the garlic cloves are golden, remove them from the pan. Add the chopped escarole and toss to coat in the oil, then add the olives, capers, and toasted pine nuts.

Increase the heat to medium and cook until all the liquid has evaporated and the escarole is dry and glistening with oil, about 15 minutes, tossing occasionally. Taste and adjust the seasoning with salt if needed. Set aside and let it cool completely.

When the potato dough has doubled in size, preheat the oven to 400°F/200°C. Generously grease a 9- or 10-inch/23 or 25 cm pie dish with olive oil.

Transfer the dough to a floured surface and divide it into 2 portions, one slightly bigger than the other. Roll out the bigger half with a rolling pin into a round big enough to cover the bottom and edges of your pie dish, then transfer it to the prepared dish, fitting it into the bottom and up the sides. Prick the bottom and sides of the dough with a fork. Add the cooled escarole filling, spreading it into an even layer.

Roll out the remaining dough into a round slightly bigger than the dish and drape it loosely over the filling. Press the edges to seal and trim the excess dough.

Drizzle generously with olive oil and brush it all over to grease the surface, then prick the dough with a fork.

Bake the escarole pie for 35 to 40 minutes, until the top is golden brown.

Serve warm or at room temperature.

Leftover escarole pie keeps well in the fridge for a couple of days. Reheat it thoroughly in a moderately hot oven before serving it.

LEFT: Escarole Pie
RIGHT: Ricotta & Broccoli Rabe Tart

torta salata con cime di rapa e ricotta

RICOTTA & BROCCOLI RABE TART

Serves 6 to 8

FOR THE PIE DOUGH

2 cups/250 g all-purpose flour

½ teaspoon fine sea salt

11½ tablespoons/160 g cold unsalted butter

Scant ½ cup/100 ml ice-cold water

FOR THE FILLING

Fine sea salt

2 large bunches of broccoli rabe (about 2 pounds/900 g total)

¼ cup/60 ml extra-virgin olive oil

1 leek, white and light green parts only, thinly sliced

1 garlic clove, minced

1 bunch of fresh mint, chopped (about ½ cup/15 g)

1 bunch of fresh parsley, chopped (about ½ cup/15 g)

¾ cup (7 ounces/200 g) whole-milk ricotta cheese, preferably sheep's milk, well drained

1½ ounces/40 g ricotta salata or Pecorino Romano cheese, finely grated (about ⅔ cup firmly packed)

1½ ounces/40 g Parmigiano Reggiano cheese, finely grated (about ⅔ cup firmly packed)

Freshly ground black pepper

-ingredients continue-

If I ask Tommaso, my husband, what he wants for dinner, nine times out of ten he'll answer: a torta salata. Savory tarts are a lifesaver—perfect for using up leftover vegetables lurking in your fridge drawer, easy to prepare ahead of time, versatile enough to be served hot or at room temperature, and great for lunchboxes the next day.

When I was growing up, my mum made a ricotta and spinach torta salata at least once a week, always encased in store-bought puff pastry. I've inherited her love for this dish, but I've given it my own spin. I make my pie dough from scratch—a flaky combination of flour, ice-cold water, and butter—and mix ricotta with whatever leafy greens are at hand. A generous handful of fresh herbs elevates the tart, adding that subtle nuance that keeps you coming back for seconds.

MAKE THE PIE DOUGH: Combine the flour and salt in a large bowl. Add the butter and toss to coat it with flour, then use a bench scraper to cut the butter lengthwise in half, then lengthwise in quarters, coating each newly cut side in flour. Dice the butter and cover each piece in flour, then keep cutting the butter and covering it in flour until all the pieces of butter are roughly the size of peas.

Add the ice-cold water little by little and mix quickly with your hands just enough to create a ball of dough without visible streaks of flour. Work the dough as little as possible.

Wrap the ball tightly in plastic wrap and refrigerate for at least 3 hours, or preferably overnight.

THE NEXT DAY, MAKE THE FILLING: Bring a large pot of water to a rolling boil and salt it generously. While the water heats, cut off the toughest stalks of the broccoli rabe and discard. Rinse the rabe under cold running water and rip it into large pieces.

Plunge the broccoli rabe into the boiling water. Submerge it with a spoon and cook until soft, about 10 minutes. Drain the broccoli rabe and let it cool until you can easily handle it. Working in batches, press the broccoli rabe into small balls that you can easily fit in your hands, squeezing well to remove any excess water. Roughly chop the rabe and set aside.

Pour the olive oil into a large skillet placed over medium-low heat and add the leek and garlic, then season with a generous pinch of salt. The salt will extract moisture from the aromatics, thus helping you cook

FOR THE TART

Softened butter, for the pie dish

All-purpose flour, for dusting

Egg wash: 1 large egg yolk beaten with a pinch of salt

down the leek without burning it. Cook the leek for about 10 minutes, stirring often, until soft.

When the leek is soft and the garlic is golden, remove the garlic from the pan, add the chopped broccoli rabe, and toss to coat in the oil.

Increase the heat to medium and cook, tossing every 5 minutes or so, until all the liquid has evaporated and the broccoli rabe is dry and glistening with oil, about 10 minutes. Taste and adjust the seasoning with salt if needed. Transfer the broccoli rabe to a large bowl and set aside to cool completely.

Mix the cooled broccoli rabe thoroughly with the mint and parsley, ricotta, ricotta salata, and Parmigiano. Taste and adjust the seasoning with salt and pepper if needed.

BAKE THE TART: Preheat the oven to 400°F/200°C. Generously butter a 9½-inch/24 cm pie dish or tart pan with or without a removable bottom.

Remove the pastry dough from the fridge and transfer it to a floured surface. Take two-thirds of the dough and roll it out with a floured rolling pin into a round big enough to cover the bottom and sides of the pie dish. Transfer it to the prepared dish, fitting it into the bottom and up the sides. Prick the bottom and sides of the dough with a fork. Add the cooled broccoli rabe filling, spreading it into an even layer.

Trim the excess dough with a knife and reserve the scraps. Pile the trimmings one on top of the other along with the remaining one-third dough and roll them out again into a rectangle about ⅛ inch/3 mm thick.

Using a sharp knife or a pastry cutter, slice the dough into even strips about ½ inch/13 mm wide. Arrange half of the strips parallel to each other across the top of the tart, spacing them evenly apart. Then take the remaining strips and carefully weave them perpendicularly over and under the first set, creating a classic lattice pattern. Trim any excess dough hanging over the edges and gently press the ends into the crust to secure them. Brush the lattice top and the edges with the egg wash.

Bake the tart for 40 to 50 minutes, until golden brown.

Set on a wire rack to cool slightly before serving.

Leftovers will keep in the fridge for a couple of days. The tart can be reheated in the oven, in the microwave, or even in a hot pan.

NOTE: Broccoli rabe, also known as rapini or cime di rapa, can be replaced by any leafy green such as spinach, chard, or even lacinato kale (cavolo nero). Make sure to boil the greens until tender, then squeeze them thoroughly, chop finely, and sauté with leeks and olive oil for an extra layer of flavor.

VARIATION:

Ricotta and Zucchini Tart

For a summer version of this tart, substitute 5 medium zucchini, thinly sliced, for the broccoli rabe. Cook the zucchini over low heat with the leek and garlic until the zucchini starts to collapse, about 20 minutes. Once cooled, mix the zucchini with 1½ cups (14 ounces/400 g) fresh ricotta, plus the mint, parsley, ricotta salata, and Parmigiano Reggiano cheese as in the broccoli rabe tart. Add 2 beaten eggs to bind the filling and the grated zest of ½ lemon for a touch of citrusy freshness.

pasta coi broccoli

PASTA WITH BROCCOLI

Serves 4 to 6

Fine sea salt

2 pounds/910 g broccoli (about 2 large heads)

½ cup/120 ml extra-virgin olive oil

4 oil-packed anchovy fillets, chopped

2 garlic cloves, minced

Red pepper flakes

FOR THE ANCHOVY BREADCRUMBS

2 tablespoons extra-virgin olive oil

2 oil-packed anchovy fillets, chopped

⅔ cup/50 g Homemade Breadcrumbs (recipe follows) or panko

TO FINISH

14 ounces/400 g short dried pasta, such as penne, fusilli, orecchiette, or rigatoni

This dish is a staple in my kitchen, not only because it sneaks in a generous portion of vegetables, but mostly because it's so good you'll find yourself stealing spoonfuls of the mushy, garlicky broccoli straight from the pan, even before the pasta goes in.

Whenever I make this dish for my cooking school students, someone always asks, How is it so creamy? Did you add cream? Is there cheese? The answer is no, no, and no. The secret is double-cooking the vegetables so that the broccoli melts into a creamy, garlicky sauce that clings perfectly to the pasta.

Bring a large pot of water to a rolling boil and salt it generously. While the water heats, clean the broccoli. Cut off the stems and divide the tops into little florets. Rinse them under running water and transfer the florets to a bowl. For any large stems, peel off the tough outer layer with a vegetable peeler and chop the pale green center. If the stems are thinner, chop them without peeling. Transfer all the stem pieces to a separate bowl.

When the water comes to a boil, add the broccoli stems and cook until they are so soft you can easily mash them on the side of the pot with a fork, about 15 minutes. Fish them out with a slotted spoon and return them to their bowl and set aside. Next, plunge the broccoli florets in the boiling water and cook them until you can easily pierce them with the tip of a knife, 8 to 10 minutes. Remove them with a slotted spoon, return them to their bowl, and set aside. Don't discard the water; you'll use it to cook the pasta, too. Top it up if needed.

Transfer the cooked broccoli stems to the cup of an immersion blender or a food processor, add ¼ cup/60 ml of the olive oil and 1 or 2 tablespoons of their cooking liquid, if too thick to puree. Puree the stems until smooth, then taste and adjust the seasoning with salt, if needed. Set aside. The broccoli puree can be made in advance and kept in an airtight container in the fridge for a couple of days.

Pour the remaining ¼ cup/60 ml olive oil into a large saucepan and add the chopped anchovies, garlic, and pepper flakes to taste (your aim is to have a warm heat that won't overpower the other flavors). Warm the oil over low heat for about 5 minutes, stirring to dissolve the anchovies. When the garlic is golden, add the broccoli florets, toss them in the garlicky oil, and cook them, stirring often, until they start to collapse and become creamy, 10 to 15 minutes. Taste and adjust the seasoning, then set aside.

MAKE THE ANCHOVY BREADCRUMBS: Pour the olive oil into a medium skillet and add the chopped anchovies. Warm the oil over low heat for about 5 minutes, stirring to dissolve the anchovies, then add the breadcrumbs and toss to coat with the oil. Increase the heat to medium-low and fry the breadcrumbs until golden and toasty, about 5 minutes. Transfer the browned breadcrumbs to a bowl and set aside.

TO FINISH: Bring the pot of water back to a rolling boil. Add the pasta and cook until al dente according to the package directions.

While the pasta is cooking, pour the broccoli stem puree into the pan with the broccoli florets and warm through over medium heat.

Drain the pasta and add it to the pan. Toss everything together, stirring energetically, so that the broccoli transforms into a creamy dressing and envelops the pasta.

Serve straight from the pan, generously sprinkling the anchovy breadcrumbs over each plate.

NOTE: The boiled broccoli florets and the stem puree can be cooked in advance and stored in an airtight container in the fridge for a couple of days, if you want a quick weeknight pasta dish.

HOMEMADE BREADCRUMBS

Homemade breadcrumbs add crunch, texture, and flavor to any dish, and they're incredibly easy to make. Cut stale bread into chunks and pulse in a food processor until you reach your desired texture, coarse or fine. Store in an airtight container at room temperature for up to 1 week.

sformato di spinaci e carote

CARROT & SPINACH FLAN

Makes 12 flans

FOR THE SPINACH

1¾ pounds/800 g fresh spinach

2 tablespoons/28 g unsalted butter

1 garlic clove, smashed and peeled

Fine sea salt and freshly ground black pepper

FOR THE CARROTS

1 pound/450 g carrots

1 bay leaf

2 tablespoons/28 g unsalted butter

1 garlic clove, smashed and peeled

Fine sea salt and freshly ground black pepper

FOR THE BESCIAMELLA

3 tablespoons/45 g unsalted butter

⅓ cup/42 g all-purpose flour

1⅔ cups/390 ml whole milk

Fine sea salt and freshly ground black pepper

Freshly grated nutmeg

-ingredients continue-

For holidays, family gatherings, or other special celebrations, try a festive sformato as the centerpiece of the meal. Even humble vegetables can be transformed into a creamy, elegant flan with the help of besciamella, cheese, and eggs.

You can make sformato throughout the year (see Note). The process is always the same: First, cook your vegetable, then chop or puree it before recooking to give it more flavor. Combine it with béchamel sauce—or ricotta for a lighter version—grated sharp cheese like Parmigiano Reggiano cheese or pecorino, and an egg, then scrape it into a mold to bake until set and golden brown.

COOK THE SPINACH: Remove the thick stems from the spinach, then rinse under running water. Transfer the still-dripping spinach to a large, deep pan. Cover and cook over medium heat until wilted, 7 to 10 minutes. If it does not fit all at once in the pan, add the spinach in large handfuls as it wilts. Transfer to a colander to drain and let it cool down until you can easily handle it. Working in batches, press the spinach into small balls that you can easily fit in your hands, squeezing them well to remove any excess water. Roughly chop the spinach and set it aside.

In a large skillet, melt the butter with the garlic over medium heat until the butter is sizzling and you can smell the garlic aroma. Add the chopped spinach and toss to coat it in the butter, then cook, stirring frequently, until the spinach is dry and glistening with butter, 7 to 10 minutes. Season to taste with salt and pepper, discard the garlic, and set aside.

COOK THE CARROTS: Peel the carrots and place them in a small pot, breaking them with your hands to make them fit if too long. Fill the pot with cold water, add the bay leaf, cover, and bring to a boil over high heat. Reduce to a simmer and cook the carrots until you can easily pierce them with a knife, 15 to 30 minutes.

Drain the carrots, discard the bay leaf, and transfer the carrots to a large plate. Mash them immediately with a fork (it's easier to do this when the carrots are still steaming hot) to get a smooth, fluffy mash.

In a large skillet, combine the butter and the garlic and set over medium heat until the butter is sizzling and you can smell the garlic aroma. Add the mashed carrots and toss to coat in the butter, then

FOR ASSEMBLY

3 tablespoons/45 g unsalted butter, for the molds

¼ cup/about 20 g Homemade Breadcrumbs (page 84) or panko, plus more for coating the molds

4 ounces/115 g Parmigiano Reggiano cheese, finely grated (about 2 cups firmly packed)

2 large eggs, lightly beaten

FOR THE PARMIGIANO REGGIANO CHEESE SAUCE

⅓ cup plus 2 tablespoons/100 ml heavy cream

3½ ounces/100 g Parmigiano Reggiano cheese, finely grated (about 1¾ cups firmly packed)

NOTE: In winter, cardoons are a treat, and a labor of love, requiring patience to clean and boil in acidulated water, but their reward is a unique flan with an artichoke flavor. Cauliflower, on the other hand, makes an incredibly delicate, gentle flan. Spring is the time for artichokes, while summer brings green beans, with onions added for a touch of sweetness. When fall arrives, squash flan becomes a festive side dish, spiced with a generous grating of nutmeg.

cook over medium heat, stirring frequently, until the carrots are dry and glistening with butter, 5 to 10 minutes. Season to taste with salt and pepper, discard the garlic, and set aside.

MAKE THE BESCIAMELLA: Melt the butter in a small saucepan over medium heat. When the butter is melted, add the flour and whisk for a few minutes until golden and toasted. Pour in the milk in a thin stream, whisking constantly to avoid lumps. Cook the besciamella for a few minutes, still stirring constantly, until thickened; your whisk should leave visible trails in the sauce. Season to taste with salt, pepper, and nutmeg. You can prepare the besciamella in advance, let it cool, and keep it in an airtight container in the fridge for up to 2 days. Gently reheat it before using.

ASSEMBLE THE FLANS: Preheat the oven to 400°F/200°C. Butter twelve ⅓-cup/80 ml molds and coat them generously with breadcrumbs. Arrange the molds on a baking sheet. If you do not have individual molds, a 12-cup standard muffin tin works just as well.

Mix the cooked spinach with half of the prepared besciamella, then add half the grated Parmigiano Reggiano cheese. Taste and adjust the seasoning with salt and pepper, then add half of the beaten eggs and mix thoroughly. Do the same with the cooked carrots.

With a spoon, fill each mold halfway with the carrot mixture. Smooth the surface and top with the spinach mixture, then sprinkle with the ¼ cup/20 g breadcrumbs.

Transfer the flans to the hot oven and bake them for 25 minutes or until firm and golden brown. Remove from the oven and let them cool down slightly.

MEANWHILE, MAKE THE PARMIGIANO REGGIANO CHEESE SAUCE: Warm the cream in a small saucepan over medium heat until simmering. Add the Parmigiano and stir until the cheese has melted and the sauce is creamy and smooth. You can prepare the cheese sauce in advance, let it cool, and keep it in an airtight container in the fridge for up to 2 days.

To serve the flans, unmold them onto a plate. If using a muffin tin, gently invert a baking sheet over the mold and flip the whole thing so the sformati fall out. Transfer to a serving dish, spoon over some Parmigiano Reggiano cheese sauce, and serve immediately.

The flans can be kept in the fridge for up to 4 days. Reheat them gently in a hot oven or in the microwave before serving them, then spoon the cheese sauce on top. If you have to reheat the cheese sauce, pour it into a small saucepan and reheat it over low heat, whisking constantly. If the sauce separates, mix in a couple of tablespoons of cream.

finocchi gratinati

FENNEL GRATIN

Serves 6 to 8 as a side dish

FOR THE FENNEL

3 large fennel bulbs (about 1 pound/450 g each)

2 tablespoons coarse sea salt

6 strips of lemon zest

1 bay leaf

¼ cup/60 ml extra-virgin olive oil

1 garlic clove, smashed and peeled

FOR THE BESCIAMELLA

3 tablespoons/45 g unsalted butter

⅓ cup/42 g all-purpose flour

1⅔ cups/390 ml whole milk

Fine sea salt and freshly ground black pepper

Freshly grated nutmeg

FOR THE FENNEL FROND PESTO

¼ cup/15 g fennel fronds

2 tablespoons hazelnuts, toasted

Fine sea salt

TO FINISH

¾ ounce/21 g Parmigiano Reggiano cheese, finely grated (about ⅓ cup firmly packed)

Extra-virgin olive oil, for drizzling

Fennel is a marvel of versatility. Raw, it's crisp and refreshing, with a texture reminiscent of a green apple and a subtle anise flavor—perfect for dipping into your finest extra-virgin olive oil or thinly sliced in a salad with segments of blood orange and meaty black olives. Roasted in wedges with a scattering of grated cheese (see page 39), it becomes caramelized and crisp. Boiled, it turns silky and buttery soft and is divine with a drizzle of olive oil and a pinch of flaky sea salt.

This recipe celebrates fennel's adaptability by combining three cooking techniques. First, the fennel is boiled until tender, then it's seared in a pan with olive oil, garlic, and lemon zest to build layers of flavor. Finally, it's baked under a comforting blanket of béchamel, topped with chopped hazelnuts and fennel fronds for added texture and vibrant color.

COOK THE FENNEL: Quarter the fennel and rinse it under running water. Bring a large pot of water to a rolling boil, then add the coarse sea salt, 3 of the lemon zest strips, and the bay leaf. Submerge the fennel quarters in the boiling water and cook them until you can easily pierce them with a knife, 20 to 25 minutes.

Drain the fennel, then rinse it quickly under cool water to hasten cooling, then divide each quarter into 2 wedges.

Have ready a 9- to 10-inch/23 to 25 cm round baking dish or ovenproof skillet.

Pour the olive oil into a large skillet, add the 3 remaining lemon zest strips and the garlic, and warm over medium heat until the garlic starts sizzling. Working in two batches, place the fennel wedges in the pan cut side down and cook them until golden brown, about 5 minutes per side. Transfer the fennel wedges to the prepared baking dish, arranging them in concentric circles.

MAKE THE BESCIAMELLA: Melt the butter in a small saucepan over medium heat. When the butter is melted, add the flour and whisk for a few minutes until golden and toasted. Pour in the milk in a thin stream, whisking constantly to avoid lumps. Cook the besciamella for a few minutes, stirring constantly, until thickened; your whisk should leave visible trails in the sauce. Season to taste with fine sea salt, pepper, and nutmeg. You can prepare the besciamella in advance, let it cool, and keep it in an airtight container in the fridge for up to 2 days. Gently reheat it before using.

MAKE THE FENNEL FROND PESTO: In a food processor, combine the fennel fronds, hazelnuts, and a pinch of fine sea salt and pulse until coarsely chopped. Set aside.

TO FINISH: Preheat the oven to 400°F/200°C. Pour the besciamella over the fennel and gently shake the baking dish so that each fennel wedge is coated and the sauce trickles down to the bottom of the dish. Sprinkle the fennel with the grated Parmigiano and drizzle with some olive oil, then transfer to the hot oven.

Bake until golden and bubbling on the edges, 25 to 30 minutes.

Dollop the fennel frond pesto over the fennel and pop the dish under the broiler for about 5 minutes, until golden brown. Keep a close eye to prevent the nuts from burning.

Serve the fennel gratin immediately.

Leftovers can be kept in an airtight container in the fridge for 3 days. Reheat in a hot oven or the microwave before serving.

VARIATION:

A Quick-Roasted Fennel with Lemon

Preheat the oven to 400°F/200°C. Halve 2 fennel bulbs vertically, place the halves cut side down, and slice them. Dress with ⅓ cup/80 ml extra-virgin olive oil, the grated zest and juice of 1 lemon, 1 minced garlic clove, and salt and pepper to taste. Scatter the fennel on a baking sheet and bake for 30 minutes, then sprinkle with ¼ cup/about 20 g grated Parmigiano Reggiano cheese and bake for 10 more minutes, until golden brown and slightly caramelized.

S-Def

ITALIANS AND OVERCOOKED VEGETABLES

"In the day and age of the al dente vegetable, what a joy to find a recipe that celebrates the well cooked, buttery vegetable."

—Fergus Henderson, *The Complete Nose to Tail*

AS ITALIANS, WE OBSESS OVER AL DENTE SPAGHETTI OR MEAT COOKED UNTIL BARELY RARE, but we generally overcook our vegetables. This is neither a chef's mistake nor the misfortune of stumbling upon a reheated side dish from the previous day. It's a deeply rooted habit of trattorie and osterie, tracing back to the way mamma and nonna cooked.

Historically, this practice stems from medieval beliefs that vegetables needed to be thoroughly cooked for safety and digestion, but it also reflects a traditional approach to cooking—vegetables were often simmered slowly in soups and stews rather than quickly sautéed. Until relatively recently, many Italian households cooked over wood or coal fires, where slow, prolonged cooking was the norm rather than the high heat of modern stovetops. Over time, this method became a way to concentrate flavors, soften tougher greens, and create comforting, well-seasoned dishes, an essential trait of cucina povera.

Traveling abroad and reading my favorite food writers, I've discovered more than one reason to appreciate—and eventually fall in love with—crisp, snappy vegetables. I have had to unlearn my habit of the Italian approach, which usually leads me to boil broccoli, cauliflower, green beans, and spinach until wilted and collapsing.

Yet there is a quiet beauty in the way Italian cooking embraces overcooked vegetables, revealing their depth of flavor and comforting textures, a charm that I feel deserves equal praise. Not all vegetables give their best when cooked for a long time—some become soggy and unpalatable—but take green beans, broccoli, zucchini, fennel, or kale: They surrender to the flame and release a relaxed, sweeter, buttery flavor that pairs beautifully with pasta dishes and meat, or even stands on its own as a comforting side dish.

When I hold summer cooking classes, I often buy large bags of beans from the market to stew (see page 51). We start the morning by trimming the beans, then transfer them to a large pot and pour in

plenty of extra-virgin olive oil, along with plum tomatoes and onions. A cup of water ensures the beans have enough moisture to stew slowly. We move the pot to the back of the stove and forget about them for more than an hour. Or, better, I tend to forget them, while my students look worried about those beans simmering away. Someone always asks, "Won't they overcook?" I have to reassure them and show them beans that have become bendy and soft, slightly wrinkled, dark green, and have shrunk to the point of surrender. This is where the magic of flavor and texture happens.

When fennel wedges are boiled until they become buttery soft and are then covered in a thick blanket of besciamella, they meld into one: silky, creamy, comforting. The same wouldn't happen if the fennel were still a bit crunchy.

The habit of overcooking vegetables often goes hand in hand with the Italian inclination for double-cooking vegetables. *Strascicare* or *ripassare* are the terms we use to describe the process of recooking boiled vegetables with plenty of extra-virgin olive oil, often elevated by the bold kick of garlic, chile pepper, or anchovies, coaxing out flavor while also achieving a luscious silken texture.

Dragging leafy vegetables through intensely flavored olive oil, shimmering with flecks of chile pepper and golden cloves of garlic, imparts flavor to the vegetables. This technique makes them perfect as a filling—such as for escarole in the Neapolitan pizza di scarola (see page 74) or broccoli rabe in the torta salata con cime di rapa e ricotta (see page 79)—but it also gives them a bold flavor that allows them to shine as side dishes.

Pasta coi broccoli (see page 83), though, is probably the best example of how overcooking and recooking vegetables can create a dish where the result is far greater than the sum of its parts. The twice-cooked broccoli collapses into a creamy sauce that clings to every strand of pasta. It's comforting, unapologetically flavorful, and a dish that embodies the soul of Italian cooking.

SAUCED

Seasonal vegetables acting as flavorful complements to pasta, rice, or gnocchi is one of the most appreciated and recognizable ways Italians use produce. From vibrant pestos to silky sauces and hearty ragùs, vegetables turn pasta into a satisfying part of any meal.

penne al pesto di rucola

ARUGULA PESTO PENNE PASTA

Makes 1¼ cups/about 300 g pesto; serves 6

FOR THE PESTO

3½ ounces/100 g fresh baby arugula (about 3½ cups packed)

¾ cup/75 g walnuts

1 garlic clove, peeled but whole

⅓ cup/80 ml extra-virgin olive oil, plus more for storing the pesto

2 ounces/56 g Parmigiano Reggiano cheese, finely grated (about 1 cup firmly packed)

Fine sea salt

FOR THE PASTA

Fine sea salt

1 pound/450 g short pasta, such as penne or tortiglioni

1 pint (10½ ounces/300 g) cherry tomatoes (about 2 cups), quartered

Handful of fresh arugula, for garnish

Handful of walnuts, toasted and roughly crushed, for garnish

Extra-virgin olive oil, for drizzling

NOTE: When making pesto, always add the grated Parmigiano Reggiano at the end, after blending all the other ingredients. That way, the cheese won't overheat and lose its delicate texture and flavor.

All you need to make this pesto is a bunch of fresh, peppery arugula, a drizzle of excellent extra-virgin olive oil—preferably with a subtle peppery note (did you know some Italian olive oils have a natural arugula flavor?)—walnuts, and a generous helping of grated Parmigiano Reggiano cheese. The ingredient list is short, but quality matters: Choose the best ingredients you can find.

This arugula pesto isn't just for pasta. It's delightful drizzled over boiled vegetables, or spread on crusty bread and topped with a soft-boiled egg and a salty anchovy for a simple yet mouthwatering appetizer or a humble, satisfying meal.

MAKE THE PESTO: Rinse the arugula under running water and dry it thoroughly using a salad spinner or a kitchen towel.

In a food processor, combine the walnuts and garlic clove and blend until the walnuts are roughly chopped. Add the arugula and olive oil and blend until the mixture becomes creamy, stopping to scrape down the sides as needed.

Transfer the arugula pesto to a bowl. Stir in the grated Parmigiano, taste, and season with salt. If not using immediately, transfer the pesto to a jar and cover it with a thin layer of olive oil to prevent oxidation. Refrigerate for up to 2 days.

COOK THE PASTA: Bring a large pot of water to a rolling boil, salt it generously, then cook the pasta until al dente according to the package directions. Reserving a few tablespoons of the pasta water, drain the pasta.

In a large serving bowl, toss the hot pasta with the arugula pesto, adding a tablespoon or two of the reserved pasta water if needed to loosen the sauce. Add the quartered cherry tomatoes and gently mix.

To serve, garnish with fresh arugula leaves, crushed walnuts, and an extra drizzle of olive oil. Serve immediately.

VARIATIONS

Pesto is wonderfully adaptable: You can blend herbs, greens, nuts, and cheese to suit the season or your taste. In winter, try lacinato kale paired with almonds. Sage and almonds make a quick aromatic dressing for pasta, too, while in summer turn to the Sicilian pesto alla Trapanese, a vibrant combination of tomatoes, almonds, basil, and pecorino.

pasta con carote, guanciale e pecorino

PASTA WITH ROASTED CARROTS, GUANCIALE & PECORINO

Serves 4

- 1 pound/450 g carrots
- ¼ cup/60 ml extra-virgin olive oil
- Fine sea salt
- Freshly ground black pepper
- A few fresh thyme sprigs
- 1 garlic clove, unpeeled
- 3½ ounces/100 g guanciale (see Note), pancetta, or lardons, cut into strips
- 14 ounces/400 g dried strand pasta, like bucatini or spaghetti
- 3½ ounces/100 g Pecorino Romano cheese, finely grated (about 1¾ cups firmly packed), plus more for serving

NOTE: Guanciale adds saltiness and crunch, but for a vegetarian version, try toasted almond slivers or crispy chickpeas for a satisfying texture.

This recipe was inspired by a pasta I had at Osteria Quattro Venti in Siena. How interesting to see carrots, so often relegated to a supporting role—whether minced to start a stew or simmered in a stock—taking center stage in a pasta dish.

This recipe turns carrots into a creamy, sweet sauce with the persistent note of caramelized garlic. Combined with sharp grated pecorino and crisp guanciale, it's like carbonara minus the eggs. When I made this for a friend who is allergic to eggs, she teared up, saying it was the first time in years she'd experienced the joy of something so reminiscent of carbonara.

Preheat the oven to 400°F/200°C.

Peel the carrots, slice them lengthwise, and arrange them on a baking sheet. Dress them with the olive oil, 1 teaspoon salt, a few turns of pepper, and the fresh thyme. Massage the carrots with the olive oil and herbs. Add the unpeeled garlic clove (the skin will protect the garlic from burning and it will result in a sweet, sticky roasted garlic clove). Transfer to the hot oven.

Roast until the carrots are slightly caramelized on the edges and easy to pierce with the tip of a knife, 35 to 45 minutes. Set them aside. The carrots can be prepared in advance and kept in the fridge for a couple of days.

Bring a large pot of water to a rolling boil and salt it not too generously, as the pecorino is already quite salty.

Meanwhile, brown the guanciale strips in a large skillet over medium heat until golden brown and crisp, about 5 minutes.

Add the pasta to the boiling water and cook until al dente according to the package directions.

While the pasta is cooking, scoop about 2 cups/500 ml of the pasta water out of the pot. Collect the roasted carrots in the jug of an immersion blender or in a food processor. Discard the thyme sprigs and squeeze the roasted garlic out of the skin. Start blending the carrots, adding the pasta water in ½-cup/120 ml increments to avoid making the puree too thin. Go for a total of about 1½ cups/354 ml pasta water. You should obtain a smooth carrot puree. Taste it and adjust with salt, if needed.

-recipe continues-

When you are almost ready to drain the pasta, pour the carrot puree into the pan with the guanciale and reheat it over medium heat.

When the pasta is ready, reserve another 1 cup/240 ml of the cooking water and then drain the pasta. Toss it into the pan with the carrot puree.

Take the pan off the heat and add the grated pecorino and a splash of pasta water. Toss and swirl the pan vigorously until the pecorino is melted and each strand of pasta is coated with the rich, creamy carrot sauce.

Serve immediately, bringing extra pecorino and pepper to the table for those who want it.

carbonara di zucchine

ZUCCHINI CARBONARA

Serves 4 as a main course

- 4 medium zucchini (about 1¾ pounds/800 g total)
- ⅓ cup/80 ml extra-virgin olive oil
- 2 garlic cloves, smashed and peeled
- Fine sea salt
- 2 large eggs
- 4 large egg yolks
- 2¼ ounces/64 g Pecorino Romano cheese, finely grated (about 1¼ cups firmly packed), plus more for serving
- 1½ ounces/43 g Parmigiano Reggiano cheese, finely grated (about ¾ cup firmly packed)
- Freshly ground black pepper
- 14 ounces/400 g rigatoni
- Fresh mint leaves, torn if too big

Some dishes in Italian cuisine have become so iconic that their recipes are treated as sacred by purists. Amatriciana must never include onions or white wine—only tomatoes and guanciale. Carbonara? Absolutely no cream, and it must feature guanciale, not pancetta.

Yet even these classic recipes were once evolving concepts rather than fixed culinary doctrines. So keep an open mind about this zucchini carbonara that offers a fresh seasonal twist on the beloved Roman classic. Crisp crescents of zucchini replace guanciale, mingling with creamy eggs, Parmigiano, and pecorino. The result is a lighter, vegetable-forward homage to the original that may one day be an icon, too.

Trim the zucchini and halve lengthwise. Very thinly slice each half crosswise into crescents and set aside.

Pour the oil into a large skillet, add the garlic, and warm over medium heat until you can smell the garlic aroma, about 2 minutes. Add the sliced zucchini and cook, stirring from time to time, until it gets soft but not mushy, and golden brown in spots, about 15 minutes. Taste and season with salt, then set aside.

Bring a large pot of water to a rolling boil and salt it not too generously, as the pecorino is already quite salty.

While the water heats, prepare the eggs for the carbonara: In a medium bowl, stir together the whole eggs, egg yolks, pecorino, Parmigiano, a pinch of salt (not too much as the pecorino is already quite salty), and lots of pepper. Whisk with a fork until you get a thick paste and set aside.

Add the pasta to the boiling water and cook until al dente according to the package directions.

When you are almost ready to drain the pasta, reheat the zucchini in the pan over medium heat.

Reserving some of the pasta water, drain the pasta and toss it into the pan with the zucchini, stirring it until it gets glossy with oil.

Take the pan off the heat and pour in the beaten egg–cheese mixture and a splash of pasta water. Toss and swirl the pan vigorously. The heat of the pasta and zucchini will work on the eggs to create a rich, creamy sauce that will coat each rigatoni.

Add a few leaves of fresh mint, and serve immediately, bringing extra pecorino and pepper to the table for those who want it.

-recipe continues-

VARIATION:

Artichoke Stem Carbonara

In winter, instead of zucchini, try the dish with artichoke stems. Prep your artichokes for cooking (see page 43 or 71), but reserve the stems; you'll need 8. Use them quickly, while they are still firm, as they tend to wither and get brownish very soon. Peel the stems until you expose the soft white part inside—this is where all the flavor is—and slice them thinly into rounds. Cook as you would the zucchini; the rest of the recipe is the same. If you cannot find artichokes with a good, firm stem, use the artichoke itself. Clean it and slice it very thinly, then cook it the same way as the zucchini or stems.

rigatoni al sugo di verdure estive

RIGATONI WITH SUMMER VEGETABLE SAUCE

Serves 6

FOR THE SAUCE

¼ cup/60 ml extra-virgin olive oil

½ small red onion, minced

Fine sea salt

1 tablespoon 'nduja (see Note)

½ small red bell pepper, diced

1 small or ½ medium zucchini, diced

½ medium eggplant, diced

2 cups/500 g tomato passata or puree

Handful of fresh basil leaves

FOR THE PASTA

Fine sea salt

1 pound/450 g dry short pasta, like rigatoni

2 tablespoons extra-virgin olive oil

⅔ cup/50 g Homemade Breadcrumbs (page 84) or panko

Grated Pecorino Romano cheese, for serving

NOTE: 'Nduja is a spicy spreadable pork sausage from Calabria that's made of ground pork and pork fat mixed with hot and sweet peppers. If you cannot find 'nduja, or if you want a vegetarian substitute, use the same quantity of chili paste.

My friend Maria Rosa came up with this sauce, and it's become one of my favorite dishes. Diced vegetables melt into a creamy tomato-based sauce with a touch of heat from the 'nduja. Topped with Pecorino Romano and crisp breadcrumbs, it's a perfect summer pasta.

This recipe makes 3 cups/750 g of sauce—more than you'll need—so save the rest for another meal. There's nothing better than pulling a jar from the freezer to bring a taste of summer to the table. It keeps in the fridge for 4 days.

MAKE THE SAUCE: Pour the olive oil into a medium saucepan, add the minced onion and a generous pinch of salt, and cook over medium-low heat until softened and translucent, about 10 minutes.

Add the 'nduja and stir it into the softened onion until it is nicely coated and the oil turns red. Cook for 1 minute. Stir in the diced pepper, zucchini, and eggplant and cook over medium heat, stirring from time to time, until all the vegetables are softened, 10 to 12 minutes.

When the vegetables have reduced to half of their initial volume, pour in the passata, reduce the heat to the lowest setting, cover, and cook until the vegetables are so soft that they can be mashed with a fork, about 20 minutes. Taste and adjust the seasoning with salt, then add a handful of basil leaves.

Blend the sauce with an immersion blender, leaving some of the diced vegetables whole to add some texture, then stir again.

COOK THE PASTA: Bring a pot of water to a rolling boil, salt it generously, and cook the pasta until al dente according to the package directions. Drain.

Heat the olive oil in a medium skillet over low heat. Add the breadcrumbs and toss to coat them with the oil. Increase the heat to medium-low and fry the breadcrumbs until golden and toasty, about 5 minutes. Transfer the browned breadcrumbs to a bowl and set aside.

Reheat 2 cups of the sauce and pour into a large bowl.

Pour the pasta into the bowl with the vegetable sauce and toss them together, stirring energetically. Stir in more sauce, if desired. Serve immediately, generously sprinkling toasted breadcrumbs and some pecorino on each plate.

HOW TO SPRUCE UP YOUR TOMATO SAUCE

WHEN MEALTIME COMES AROUND AND THERE'S NOTHING READY TO EAT, you can always improvise dinner if you have a package of dried pasta and a can of tomatoes in your pantry. Starting with crushed peeled tomatoes or tomato passata (or puree), spruce it up with your favorite pantry ingredients or fresh vegetables, and you'll have an easy, nourishing meal ready in no time. Here are some of my favorite suggestions.

PASTA AL POMODORO: For the most basic tomato sauce, all you need is tomato passata, a fat, and an aromatic. Use butter and onion with your tomato passata, like they do in northern Italy. Opt for extra-virgin olive oil and garlic, and you'll be eating like a Tuscan. Prefer olive oil and onion? You might just have southern Italian roots.

My pasta al pomodoro is made with spaghetti cooked al dente and tossed in a tomato sauce prepared with plenty of extra-virgin olive oil, a crushed clove of garlic, tomato passata, and a single basil leaf for a fresh, balsamic note.

PASTA ALLA PUTTANESCA: A hymn to pantry staples, this punchy pasta dish can be whipped up in less than 20 minutes—just the time it takes to cook your pasta. It's made with simple, affordable ingredients like canned tomatoes, capers, anchovies, and olives.

You'll let garlic, anchovy fillets, and red pepper flakes gently release their aroma in olive oil. Add canned crushed peeled tomatoes to the pan and simmer them into a sauce before olives and capers join the mix for an extra hit of flavor. To me, the perfect puttanesca sauce clings best to al dente spaghetti.

SUGO AL TONNO E POMODORO: This is one of my mum's go-to pasta sauces, and now it's become a staple in my weekly meal rotation. Choose your favorite pasta—I prefer short shapes with a hole to catch the sauce, like penne or tortiglioni—and pair it with a can of high-quality tuna, a can of tomato puree, a white onion, a touch of chile heat, and, of course, extra-virgin olive oil. Start by gently sweating thinly sliced onions in olive oil with a pinch of red pepper flakes. Add the tuna and tomato puree, then let it simmer for about 15 minutes, until the sauce becomes thick and glossy.

pici alla segale con zucca, porri e salsiccia

RYE PICI PASTA WITH BUTTERNUT SQUASH, LEEKS & SAUSAGES

Serves 4 to 6 as a first course

FOR THE SQUASH, LEEK, AND SAUSAGE SAUCE

- 2 medium leeks, white and light green parts only
- ½ cup/120 ml extra-virgin olive oil, plus more as needed
- Fine sea salt
- 8 ounces/225 g fresh Italian sausages, casings removed, crumbled into small pieces
- 1½ pounds/700 g butternut squash, peeled, seeded, and diced
- 12 fresh sage leaves

FOR THE PICI

- 2½ cups/320 g tipo "00" flour or all-purpose flour
- ¾ cup/80 g rye flour
- 1 teaspoon extra-virgin olive oil, plus more for brushing
- ½ teaspoon fine sea salt
- ½ cup/90 g semolina flour, plus more for dusting

TO FINISH

- Fine sea salt
- Grated Pecorino Romano, for serving

During the fall, squash becomes a centerpiece in my cooking—roasted and pureed into velvety soup, or sautéed and tossed with pasta as in this dish.

The sauce for pici, the beloved hand-pulled, hand-rolled pasta of Tuscany, incorporates slender leeks, butternut squash, piquant Pecorino Romano, and fresh sausages. To give the dish an even more rustic appeal, I like to replace part of the all-purpose flour with rye flour when making pici. The rye adds a subtle nuttiness and a brownish hue to the pasta.

MAKE THE SQUASH, LEEK, AND SAUSAGE SAUCE: Slice the leeks lengthwise and rinse under running water to remove any soil. Thinly slice them crosswise.

Pour ¼ cup/60 ml of the olive oil into a large skillet, then add the leeks and a generous pinch of salt to help them soften without burning. Sauté the leeks over low heat, stirring occasionally, until the leeks reduce to one-third of their original volume and become soft and creamy, about 30 minutes. Transfer to a small bowl and set aside.

In the same skillet, add the crumbled sausage and cook over medium heat until golden brown and crisp, 5 to 8 minutes. If the sausage starts to stick, add a tablespoon of olive oil to the pan. Transfer the sausage and its fat to the bowl with the leeks.

Return the skillet to the heat, add the remaining ¼ cup/60 ml olive oil, the diced squash, and sage leaves. Season with salt and cook over medium heat, stirring occasionally, until the squash is cooked through, tender, and beginning to collapse, about 20 minutes.

Mash some of the squash with the back of a wooden spoon to create a creamier texture. Return the leeks and sausage to the skillet, mix well, taste, and adjust the seasoning with salt if needed. Set aside.

MAKE THE PICI: In a large bowl, combine the "00" flour and rye flour. Add ¾ cup plus 1 tablespoon/200 ml water, the olive oil, and salt, stirring with a fork until the dough comes together in crumbly pieces. Transfer to a clean work surface and press the crumbs into a cohesive ball.

Knead the dough by hand—about 10 minutes. It is ready when the dough feels smooth, silky, and slightly springy. Pici dough texture is closer to bread dough than to egg pasta dough. If the dough feels too

NOTE: Fresh pici are best cooked immediately after they're made; if you hold them at room temperature they might stick together. However, they freeze beautifully. If you want to prepare the pici in advance, spread the fresh pasta on a large baking sheet dusted with semolina flour, freeze until firm, then transfer to a zip-top freezer bag. They'll keep in the freezer for up to 3 months. Cook straight from frozen, adding an extra 2 minutes to the cooking time.

dry and stiff, add a few drops of water. (Alternatively, knead in a stand mixer fitted with the dough hook for 5 minutes on low speed, then finish kneading by hand for 5 more minutes.)

Cover the dough with an overturned bowl or a damp kitchen towel and let it rest for 30 minutes at room temperature.

Place the semolina flour in a small bowl, then dust a baking sheet generously with additional semolina flour.

With a rolling pin, roll out the dough to a ¼-inch/6 mm thickness. Brush the surface lightly with olive oil to prevent it from drying out. Using a sharp knife or pizza cutter, cut the dough into strips ¼ inch/6 mm wide. Work with only one strip of dough at a time, because if you cut multiple strips at once, they will stick together and become difficult to work with. To form the pici, take one strip and anchor one end with your hand. Roll and stretch the strip with your other hand into a long, thick chubby noodle, slightly thicker than a bucatino. Drop the picio (singular for pici) into the semolina flour, coil it loosely around your hand, stretch it gently, and place it on the prepared baking sheet. Repeat until you've used up all the dough.

TO FINISH: Bring a large pot of water to a rolling boil and salt it generously. Add the pici and cook for 5 to 6 minutes, until just al dente. Pici have a dense, chewy texture; do not overcook them. Reserving ½ cup/120 ml of the pasta water, drain the pici.

While the pici cook, reheat the squash, leek, and sausage sauce over medium heat.

Add the reserved pasta water to loosen and bring the sauce together. Add the drained pici and toss them directly into the sauce. Stir well to coat the pasta evenly.

Serve immediately with a generous sprinkle of grated Pecorino Romano.

Any leftovers can be stored in an airtight container in the fridge for up to 3 days. Reheat in a skillet over medium heat, adding a few spoonfuls of water to restore the creamy texture.

LEFT: Potato Gnocchi with Radicchio & Gorgonzola Cheese
RIGHT: Rye Pici Pasta with Butternut Squash, Leeks & Sausages

gnocchi con radicchio e gorgonzola

POTATO GNOCCHI WITH RADICCHIO & GORGONZOLA CHEESE

Serves 4 to 6 as a first course, or 4 as a main course

FOR THE GNOCCHI

1 pound/450 g russet potatoes, ideally of similar size (about 1 large or 2 medium)

1 teaspoon fine sea salt

Pinch of freshly grated nutmeg

2 tablespoons lightly beaten egg (about ½ large egg)

⅔ cup plus 1 tablespoon/91 g all-purpose flour, plus more for rolling

FOR THE RADICCHIO SAUCE

2 tablespoons extra-virgin olive oil

½ yellow onion (about 4 ounces/115 g), finely minced

Fine sea salt

1 head radicchio di Chioggia (about 12 ounces/340 g), quartered and finely shredded

3 fresh thyme sprigs, leaves picked

Freshly ground black pepper

5 ounces/150 g Gorgonzola cheese, cut into pieces

I used to dislike gnocchi—too gummy, too heavy—until I learned to make them from scratch. Now there's no going back. Homemade gnocchi are tender and pillowy, a world apart from their store-bought counterparts. The key lies in cooking the potatoes properly—either steaming or boiling them whole with their skins on to minimize moisture absorption. Once cooked, let them cool completely to release any trapped steam, ensuring a light dough.

Fresh homemade gnocchi call for a creamy, cheesy sauce. Here sautéed radicchio and toasted walnuts are brought together with a generous spoonful of Gorgonzola for a cozy winter meal.

MAKE THE GNOCCHI: Scrub the potatoes clean under cold running water and place them in a medium saucepan. Cover with cold water and bring to a boil over high heat. Once boiling, reduce the heat to a simmer and cook the potatoes until you can easily pierce them with a knife—this will depend on their size, so check them periodically.

While still warm, peel the potatoes, using a clean kitchen towel to hold them if they're too hot to handle. Pass the peeled potatoes through a ricer or food mill onto a wooden board or clean work surface. Spread them out gently to let the steam escape; this step ensures the potatoes stay dry, requiring less flour in the dough.

Once the potatoes have cooled completely, sprinkle them with the salt and nutmeg. Drizzle the beaten egg over the potatoes, then gradually add the flour. Using a fork, gently mash the potatoes on the board and mix the ingredients until they start to come together.

Gather the potatoes into a cohesive ball and knead briefly, just until the dough is soft and smooth. Avoid overworking it—kneading too much will make the gnocchi dense and heavy. The dough should be pliable and slightly wet to the touch, but not sticky. Form it into a ball and set it aside. Clean your work surface with a bench scraper or spatula to remove any excess bits of dough.

Dust a baking sheet lightly with flour. Divide the dough into 8 portions and roll each into a rope about ⅔ inch/1.5 cm thick. Cut the rope into pieces slightly larger than a hazelnut. You can leave the gnocchi as they are, small chubby pillows, or round each piece of dough into a ball. For ridged gnocchi, press each piece of dough against a gnocchi

TO FINISH

Fine sea salt

Grated Parmigiano Reggiano cheese, for serving

¼ cup/25 g walnuts, toasted and roughly chopped

board or the back of a fork. Push down firmly, then drag and roll the dough along the tines to create grooves on one side and an indent on the other. These ridges and dimples are perfect for holding sauces.

Transfer to the prepared baking sheet and repeat with the remaining dough. You can boil the gnocchi immediately or store them in the fridge for a few hours.

MAKE THE RADICCHIO SAUCE: Warm the olive oil in a large skillet over medium heat. Add the onion and a generous pinch of salt to help soften it and prevent burning. Cook the onion, stirring often, until soft and translucent, about 5 minutes.

Add the radicchio and season with salt. Stir well, cover, and cook over medium-low heat, stirring occasionally, until the radicchio wilts and transforms from vibrant purple to a deep burgundy, 10 to 12 minutes.

Stir in the thyme leaves and adjust the seasoning with salt and pepper. Reduce the heat to its minimum setting, then add the Gorgonzola. Stir gently until it melts into a creamy sauce.

TO FINISH: Bring a large pot of water to a rolling boil and salt it generously. Working in batches to avoid overcrowding, add the gnocchi and cook until they float to the top, 3 to 5 minutes. Remove them with a spider or slotted spoon, letting the excess water drip off.

Transfer the gnocchi directly into the skillet with the radicchio and Gorgonzola sauce. Toss gently to coat, letting the gnocchi absorb the sauce and its flavors.

Serve immediately, sprinkled generously with grated Parmigiano and scattered with toasted walnuts for a delightful crunch.

risotto con finferli e castagne

CHANTERELLE & CHESTNUT RISOTTO

Serves 4 to 6 as a first course

FOR THE STOCK

- ⅔ packed cup (¾ ounce/20 g) dried porcini mushrooms (shiitake can be used as an alternative)
- About 5 cups/1.2 L steaming-hot water
- 2 teaspoons fine sea salt
- 6 fresh sage leaves
- 1 fresh rosemary sprig
- 3 juniper berries (optional), lightly crushed

FOR THE RISOTTO

- 5 tablespoons/70 g unsalted butter
- 1 small yellow onion (about 4 ounces/120 g), minced
- Fine sea salt
- 1¾ cups/350 g Carnaroli rice (Arborio would do as well)
- ½ cup/120 ml dry white wine
- 1 pound/450 g chanterelles (see Note), cleaned and quartered
- 2 ounces/56 g Parmigiano Reggiano cheese, finely grated (about 1 cup firmly packed), plus more for serving
- 3½ ounces/100 g cooked and peeled chestnuts, or packed steamed chestnuts, crumbled
- Freshly ground black pepper

A good risotto starts with a well-made stock, and while classic versions often rely on meat-based broths—like chicken or beef—or a simple vegetable stock, Italians also turn to more flavorful, plant-based alternatives. Here dried porcini mushrooms are steeped in hot water along with sage and rosemary, creating a heady stock with woody, undergrowth aromas that perfectly complement chanterelles and chestnuts. This technique not only maximizes the deep umami of mushrooms but also makes the most of a single ingredient in true Italian fashion.

MAKE THE STOCK: Place the dried porcini mushrooms in a saucepan with the steaming-hot water. Add the salt, sage leaves, rosemary, and juniper berries (if using). Let this steep for about 30 minutes, allowing the water to absorb the aromatic notes of mushrooms and herbs to create a flavorful stock.

Scoop the soaked mushrooms out of the stock, squeezing any excess liquid back into the pan, finely chop the mushrooms, and set them aside. Discard the herbs and juniper berries and keep the stock warm over low heat.

MAKE THE RISOTTO: Melt half of the butter in a large saucepan over low heat. Add the minced onion and ½ teaspoon salt, stirring gently until the onion becomes translucent and soft, about 5 minutes. Be careful not to brown it; this base should be delicate and sweet.

Increase the heat to medium-low and add the rice. Toast the rice for about 5 minutes, stirring constantly, until the grains turn translucent, almost pearly, and emit a faint, crackling sound. To check if it's properly toasted, pick up a few grains: They should feel scorching hot to the touch.

Pour in the white wine and stir until it has evaporated completely. Begin adding the warm stock one ladleful at a time, stirring frequently and allowing each addition to be absorbed before adding more. This slow process helps the rice release its starch, creating the creamy texture risotto is known for.

After 10 minutes, stir in the chopped porcini mushrooms and the chanterelles. Continue cooking, adding stock as needed, until the

NOTE: If chanterelles aren't available, fresh porcini make an excellent substitute without requiring any adjustments to the recipe. Alternatively, you can use honey mushrooms, oyster mushrooms, cremini, or shiitake. For best results, sauté the mushrooms separately in a generous knob of butter over medium-high heat until browned—this step enhances the depth of their flavor.

rice is creamy but still slightly al dente. You might not use all the stock. (Adjust the cooking time if using a different rice variety like Arborio.)

Remove the pan from the heat and immediately stir in the remaining butter, the grated Parmigiano, and crumbled chestnuts. Stir vigorously to cream the butter and Parmigiano into the rice, giving it a rich, velvety texture. Taste and adjust the seasoning with salt and pepper.

To check the consistency, ladle a small amount of risotto onto a plate. Tap the bottom of the plate; the risotto should spread gently. If it's too thick, add a bit more stock.

Bring the saucepan to the table and serve the risotto immediately, with extra grated Parmigiano Reggiano cheese on the side for those who want to pile on a little more.

cavatelli al ragù di lenticchie e zucca

CAVATELLI WITH PUMPKIN & LENTIL RAGÙ

Makes 5 to 6 cups/1.5 to 1.8 kg ragù; serves 4 to 6

FOR THE LENTIL RAGÙ

¾ ounce/20 g dried porcini mushrooms (shiitake can be used as an alternative)

3¼ cups/750 ml hot water

1 small carrot, finely chopped

1 celery stalk, finely chopped

1 medium leek, white and light green parts only, finely sliced

1 small yellow onion (about 3½ ounces/100 g), finely chopped

4 fresh sage leaves, finely chopped

1 fresh rosemary sprig, leaves picked and finely chopped

1 garlic clove, finely chopped

¼ cup/60 ml extra-virgin olive oil

1 bay leaf

Fine sea salt

Red pepper flakes (optional)

2 tablespoons tomato paste

7 ounces/200 g pumpkin, or any other winter squash, peeled, seeded, and cut into ⅓-inch/1 cm dice

1 cup (7 ounces/200 g) green lentils, rinsed

½ cup/120 ml red wine

14 ounces/400 g canned peeled tomatoes, crushed with your hands

Freshly ground black pepper

-ingredients continue-

This lentil ragù, hearty and satisfying without any meat, is proof that vegetarian sauces can stand proudly alongside their meaty counterparts. Lentils provide the backbone, while the addition of finely chopped vegetables builds layers of flavor. Pumpkin melts into a creamy sweetness, giving the sauce its velvety texture. A generous spoonful of tomato paste and dried porcini add umami and depth, while crushed tomatoes transform it into a sauce that clings beautifully to any pasta, fresh or dried.

You can serve lentil ragù with store-bought pasta, but if you have the time, make the cavatelli yourself. The fresh pasta boasts a chewy texture that pairs seamlessly with the rich lentil ragù, its ridged surface absorbing every bit of flavor.

MAKE THE LENTIL RAGÙ: Start by soaking the dried porcini mushrooms in a bowl with the hot water. Let them steep while you prepare the base of the ragù.

In a large heavy-bottomed pot, combine the carrot, celery, leek, onion, sage and rosemary leaves, and garlic. Pour in the olive oil and add the bay leaf, along with a generous pinch of salt. For a touch of heat, add a pinch of pepper flakes. Cook the mixture slowly over low heat, stirring occasionally, until the vegetables are soft, fragrant, and meltingly tender, about 20 minutes.

Stir in the tomato paste and let it caramelize for 2 minutes over medium heat, enhancing its umami richness. Add the diced pumpkin, stirring well to coat it in the aromatic base. Cook, stirring from time to time, until the pumpkin begins to soften and collapse around the edges, 8 to 10 minutes.

Remove the soaked mushrooms from their water, squeezing out any excess liquid. Reserve the soaking water and chop the mushrooms finely. Add them to the pot along with the lentils, stirring to mix them thoroughly. Pour in the red wine and let it cook for 5 minutes, or until the alcohol has evaporated.

Pour 2 cups/480 ml of the reserved mushroom soaking water into the pot, then add the crushed tomatoes. Stir to mix, cover, and bring to a gentle simmer. Let the ragù cook over low heat, checking occasionally to ensure the lentils don't dry out, until the lentils are tender and almost melting into the sauce, 50 minutes to 1 hour. If needed, add more of the

FOR THE CAVATELLI

2¼ cups/400 g semolina flour, plus more for dusting

TO FINISH

Fine sea salt

Grated Parmigiano Reggiano cheese, for serving

NOTES:

- If you do not want to cook the cavatelli immediately, you can freeze them by placing them in a single layer on a baking sheet generously dusted with semolina flour. Once frozen, transfer to a zip-top bag and store for up to 3 months. Alternatively, let the cavatelli dry on the tray for up to a day before cooking.
- This recipe makes a double batch of ragù. Keep it in an airtight container in the fridge for up to 5 days or freeze it for up to 3 months.

mushroom water to maintain a thick, saucy consistency. Taste the ragù toward the end of cooking and adjust the seasoning with salt and black pepper.

MEANWHILE, MAKE THE CAVATELLI: Pour the semolina flour into a large bowl, add ¾ cup plus 1 tablespoon/200 ml water and, using a fork, stir until the dough comes together in crumbly pieces. Transfer to a clean work surface and press the crumbs into a cohesive ball.

Knead the dough by hand—about 10 minutes. It is ready when the dough feels smooth, silky, and slightly springy. Semolina dough texture is closer to bread dough than to egg pasta dough. (Alternatively, knead in a stand mixer fitted with the dough hook for 5 minutes on low speed, then finish kneading by hand for 5 more minutes.)

Cover the dough with an overturned bowl or a damp kitchen towel and let it rest for 30 minutes at room temperature.

When ready to make the cavatelli, prepare a tray dusted with semolina flour to hold the shaped cavatelli.

Cut off a small piece of dough and keep the remaining dough covered to prevent drying. Roll the piece into a rope about ⅜ inch/1 cm in diameter. Using a knife, cut the rope into small pillows about ⅜ inch/1 cm long—each piece should be slightly smaller than a chickpea.

To shape the cavatelli, use the round, blunt tip of a knife or a bench scraper. Push each dough pillow down and toward yourself, allowing it to curl around the blade and form its characteristic shape. If you have a ridged gnocchi board, shape the cavatelli directly on the board to imprint them with a fun ridged pattern that enhances their ability to hold on to the sauce.

Flick the shaped cavatelli onto the prepared tray. Repeat with the remaining dough until all the cavatelli are formed.

TO FINISH: Bring a large pot of water to a rolling boil and salt it generously. Add the cavatelli and cook for 5 to 6 minutes, until just al dente.

Reserving 1 cup/240 ml of the pasta water, drain the cavatelli and toss them in a bowl with half of the prepared lentil ragù. If the pasta looks too dry, gradually add some reserved pasta water while tossing energetically to create a silky, creamy sauce.

Finish with a generous sprinkle of grated Parmigiano Reggiano cheese and serve immediately.

A RISOTTO FOR ALL SEASONS

RISOTTO IS THE ULTIMATE COMFORT FOOD. It can shine as a festive Sunday meal or come together quickly as a weeknight fix, as often all you need to make a good risotto is already in your pantry and in your fridge.

Learning the basics—the ingredients and techniques behind a perfect risotto—is well worth the effort. Once you master them, you can improvise with seasonal ingredients and truly make the recipe your own.

FAT: In the north of Italy, where risotto originates, rice is traditionally toasted in butter. However, in other parts of Italy, such as in Tuscany, famed for its olive groves, you'll more likely find extra-virgin olive oil as the cooking fat of choice, and it's the method I personally prefer.

RICE: Several Italian rice varieties work beautifully for risotto, all characterized by their round, plump grains and excellent absorbent qualities, allowing them to soak up the flavors of the fat, stock, and other ingredients. My go-to is Carnaroli, the king of Italian rice, prized for its high starch content and creamy texture. Arborio and Vialone Nano are excellent alternatives.

STOCK: Stock is the unsung hero of a good risotto. It's what cooks the rice and infuses every grain with flavor, making it plump and creamy. So never compromise on its quality: A bad stock can ruin even the best intentions. A simple, honest homemade vegetable stock works wonders, especially when you add a couple of Parmigiano Reggiano cheese rinds to the vegetables and simmer the stock for 2 hours over low heat. Sometimes I pare down the flavors, using an aromatic stock made with herbs, as in the Chanterelle and Chestnut Risotto (page 117). Tomato water, saved when making Tuscan Tomato Sauce (page 221), is ideal for a tomato risotto or for a creamy risotto laced with grated Parmigiano Reggiano cheese and fried eggplant.

VEGETABLES: The Chanterelle and Chestnut Risotto (page 117) is a great starting point for any vegetable-based risotto. To keep the vegetables fresh and vibrant, add them halfway through the cooking process. For heartier vegetables like radicchio, kale, or artichokes, briefly sauté them, just enough to wilt or soften, before adding them to the risotto. You can also try fried eggplant cubes for a summery risotto.

For butternut squash, you have two options: Cube and sauté it or bake the halved squash (see Roasted Squash, page 173) and scoop the roasted pulp directly into the risotto for a creamy, orange-hued, comforting result. The same can be done with tomatoes: Roast them, blend them into a creamy sauce, and stir the sauce into the risotto (see Roasted Tomato Orzotto, page 165).

Tender vegetables, such as shaved asparagus, thinly sliced zucchini, zucchini blossoms, fresh fava beans, or peas, as well as flavorful mushrooms like porcini and chanterelles, can be added raw to the risotto during the last 10 minutes of cooking.

HERBS, NUTS, AND OTHER ADDITIONS: Incorporate fresh herbs for added vibrancy and freshness: Pair mint with zucchini or asparagus, thyme or calamint with mushrooms, sage with squash, and basil with tomatoes or eggplants. For crunch, sprinkle a handful of nuts or seeds: Toasted hazelnuts or pumpkin seeds are perfect with squash, walnuts with radicchio, and almonds with eggplants. If you'd like to add a touch of richness, try thin strips of golden-brown pancetta or bits of crumbled sausage.

Be careful not to overdo it, though. Simply choosing just one vegetable and finishing the risotto with butter and a cheese that complements it will make for a winning combination.

FRIED & GRILLED

High heat can bring out the best in vegetables. Grilling the Italian way often means in a grill pan on the stovetop, which intensifies the sweetness of vegetables and adds light char without the need for outdoor cooking. Frying gives veg an irresistible crispiness.

frittata con asparagi grigliati

GRILLED ASPARAGUS FRITTATA

Serves 2 as a main course, 4 as an appetizer

FOR THE GRILLED ASPARAGUS

1 pound/450 g asparagus

2 tablespoons extra-virgin olive oil

1 tablespoon fresh lemon juice

1 garlic clove, smashed and peeled

12 fresh mint leaves, sliced into thin ribbons

Fine sea salt and freshly ground black pepper

FOR THE FRITTATA

4 large eggs

2 tablespoons grated Parmigiano Reggiano cheese, plus more for serving

Fine sea salt and freshly ground black pepper

2 tablespoons extra-virgin olive oil

Fresh mint leaves, torn

Grilling asparagus brings out the vegetable's bold, verdant flavor, with just enough char to lend complexity. Slightly tender but still with a satisfying bite, it makes a perfect side to scrambled or soft-boiled eggs and is an irresistible seasonal addition to a frittata.

This asparagus frittata is great for brunch or dinner and it shines at picnics or in a lunchbox, tucked into a sandwich with crisp lettuce and a smear of mustard or mayonnaise.

GRILL THE ASPARAGUS: Prepare the asparagus by snapping off the tough, woody ends. Rinse the spears thoroughly. Slice any thicker spears lengthwise, leaving the slender ones whole. Place them in a large bowl and dress with the olive oil, lemon juice, garlic, and sliced mint. Toss gently to coat and let marinate for about 30 minutes.

Heat a cast-iron grill pan over high heat. To test if it's hot enough, sprinkle a few drops of water into the pan—if they bounce and evaporate quickly, it's ready.

Grill the asparagus in batches until tender, slightly bendy, and charred in spots, about 3 minutes. Transfer to a plate and season with salt and pepper.

MAKE THE FRITTATA: In a bowl, beat the eggs until smooth. Add the grated Parmigiano and season with a generous pinch of salt and several turns of pepper.

Place a 9- or 10-inch/23 or 25 cm nonstick skillet over medium-high heat. Pour in the olive oil and heat until it shimmers. Arrange the grilled asparagus in a single layer in the pan. Pour the egg mixture evenly over the asparagus and gently shake the pan to distribute it. Scatter torn mint leaves over the surface.

Cook the frittata over medium heat until the edges are set, the bottom is golden, and the top is still slightly wet, 6 to 8 minutes.

Invert a large plate over the pan and, in one quick motion, flip the frittata onto the plate. Return the pan to the stove, slide the frittata back into the pan, and cook for another 2 to 3 minutes, until fully set.

Slide the frittata onto a serving plate, flipping it so the nicest side with the neatly lined-up asparagus faces up. Sprinkle with more grated Parmigiano and serve immediately.

Store leftover frittata in an airtight container in the fridge for up to 2 days. Reheat gently before serving—or enjoy it cold for a quick meal.

frittelle di fiori di zucca

ZUCCHINI FLOWER FRITTERS

Makes 12 fritters

20 zucchini flowers (see Note)

2 small zucchini (about 5 ounces/150 g total)

Fine sea salt

1 ounce/28 g Parmigiano Reggiano cheese, finely grated (about ½ cup firmly packed)

1 garlic clove, finely grated or minced

1 tablespoon finely chopped fresh basil

½ cup/63 g all-purpose flour

1 cup/240 ml high-heat vegetable oil, such as sunflower or peanut

NOTE: If zucchini flowers are unavailable, thinly sliced zucchini (about 2 ounces/56 g) can be used as a substitute. However, try to find blossoms when in season, as their unique floral flavor adds something truly special.

Bright as the summer sun, with a delicate floral scent, zucchini flowers herald summer feasts. You can fry them whole in a crisp batter (see page 130), stuff them with mozzarella and anchovies, or shred them to make these savory, herby fritters that hail from Calabria. These are the perfect appetizer for a garden party spread, especially when paired with Eggplant Croquettes (page 69).

Prepare the zucchini flowers by removing the pistils and stems, then slicing the flowers into 4 to 5 thin strips. Grate the zucchini on the large holes of a box grater and transfer it to a large bowl along with the flower strips. Sprinkle with 1 teaspoon salt and set aside for about 1 hour.

Once the grated zucchini and flowers have released their moisture, squeeze them gently in the bowl to remove excess water, but do not discard the liquid—keep it there with the zucchini—it will become part of the batter.

Add the grated Parmigiano, garlic, and basil to the bowl. Gradually incorporate the flour, stirring until the batter is thick, cohesive, and no longer watery. Depending on the amount of water released, you might not need all of the flour. Taste and adjust with more salt if needed.

Line a plate with paper towels and keep it near the stove. Pour the oil into a large pot and set over medium-high heat. When the oil registers 350°F/175°C on a deep-frying thermometer, or when the handle of a wooden spoon dipped in the oil is immediately surrounded by tiny bubbles, you're ready to fry.

Working in two batches to avoid overcrowding, drop a heaping tablespoon of batter gently into the hot oil for each fritter. Cook, turning them occasionally, until golden brown and crisp, about 5 minutes. Transfer the fritters to the paper towels to drain.

Serve hot or at room temperature.

Leftover fritters can be stored in the fridge for up to 2 days. Reheat gently in a hot oven or microwave before serving.

fritto misto di verdure

FRIED VEGETABLE PLATTER

Serves 4 to 6 as an appetizer

½ medium eggplant (about 6 ounces/ 180 g)

1 small zucchini (about 4½ ounces/ 125 g)

Fine sea salt

1 carrot

1 small potato (about 5 ounces/ 150 g)

1 small yellow onion (about 3 ounces/ 85 g)

12 zucchini flowers

12 fresh sage leaves

FOR THE BEER BATTER

2¾ cups/ 345 g all-purpose flour, plus more as needed

¾ cup/ 180 ml cold sparkling water

1 cup/ 240 ml cold pale lager beer, such as Birra Moretti, plus more as needed

2 teaspoons fine sea salt

Freshly ground black pepper

TO FINISH

4¼ cups/ 1 L high-heat vegetable oil, such as sunflower or peanut

1 lemon, cut into wedges

Flaky sea salt

Remote Italian trattorias are where you can have some of the most memorable dining experiences. Tucked away in the countryside, these trattorias are often frequented by local workers or adventurous travelers, and the menus are a testament to their relationship with the nearby farmers and producers.

Whenever I dine at one, I search the menu for the four magical words: *fritto misto di verdure*. This colorful platter evolves with the seasons, featuring an array of vegetables delicately sliced and encased in a crisp, airy beer batter. When you make it at home, you can tailor the recipe to the season, mixing and matching vegetables, or keep it simple with just a few standouts, such as zucchini blossoms and sage leaves.

Rinse the eggplant and slice it crosswise into paper-thin slices about 1⁄10 inch/1 mm thick. Do the same with the zucchini. Set a colander over a bowl, then layer the eggplant and zucchini slices in the colander, sprinkling some fine sea salt between the layers. Set aside for 30 minutes.

Peel the carrot and slice it on the bias into paper-thin slices about 1⁄10 inch/1 mm thick. Transfer to a small bowl. Peel the potato and slice it into paper-thin slices. Place the slices in a bowl of cold water.

Peel the onion and slice it crosswise into rounds ¼ inch/6 mm thick, then separate them into rings. Put them aside in another bowl.

Clean the zucchini flowers by discarding their pistils. Set the blossoms aside. Rinse and pat the sage leaves dry.

After 30 minutes, when a brownish liquid has gathered at the bottom of the eggplant and zucchini bowl, gently squeeze the vegetables to remove the excess moisture and pat them dry with paper towels.

PREPARE THE BEER BATTER: In a bowl, mix the flour with the sparkling water, then add the beer and whisk to remove any lumps. Season it with the salt and pepper. It should have the texture of runny yogurt. Dip a carrot slice in the batter and gently shake off the excess—most of the batter should slip off, leaving a light coating that clings to the carrot.

-recipe continues-

If the batter is too thick, add a few drops of beer. If it's too runny, stir in an extra tablespoon of flour. When you're happy with the texture, refrigerate the batter while you heat the oil for frying; the batter works best when cold.

TO FINISH: Set a wire rack on a baking sheet and keep it near the stove. Pour 3 inches/about 7 cm of vegetable oil into a large, deep pan and set over medium-high heat. Preheat the oven to 200°F/100°C.

When the oil registers 350°F/175°C on a deep-frying thermometer, or when the handle of a wooden spoon dipped in the oil is immediately surrounded by tiny bubbles, you can start frying the vegetables.

Starting with the eggplant and zucchini, dip them in the batter using kitchen tongs, shake them to remove excess batter, and then plunge them into the hot oil. Fry, turning them once to get them crisp and golden on both sides, 2 to 3 minutes. Transfer the fried vegetables to the wire rack, then transfer the whole setup to the oven to keep warm.

Fry the remaining vegetables (except the potatoes) in batches, allowing the oil to return to temperature between batches and transferring each batch of vegetables to the wire rack in the oven.

Finally, drain the potatoes, pat them dry, and fry them without batter until golden, 2 to 3 minutes.

When all of the vegetables have been fried, transfer them to a platter, add the lemon wedges, and sprinkle with flaky sea salt. Serve immediately while still warm.

TIPS AND TRICKS FOR A GREAT FRIED VEGETABLE PLATTER

I'VE NOTICED A COMMON HESITATION AMONG MY COOKING SCHOOL STUDENTS: the fear of frying. Yet, when done correctly, frying can be extremely rewarding, especially when the result is a beautiful platter of fried vegetables. To help you master the art, here are my top tips for frying with confidence:

- **VENT IT:** Turn on your vent fan a few minutes before you start frying to help minimize that lingering deep-fried smell.
- **FRY IN HOT OIL:** Hot oil is essential for crisp results. If the oil is not hot enough, your vegetables will absorb it and turn soggy. Aim for 350°F/175°C, using a deep-frying thermometer to check. No thermometer? Dip the handle of a wooden spoon or chopstick into the oil; if it's immediately surrounded by tiny bubbles, you're ready to fry.
- **USE TWO PAIRS OF TONGS:** Keep one pair for dipping vegetables into the batter and a clean pair for turning and removing the veg from the hot oil. Kitchen tweezers are an option, too—they're precise and versatile.
- **PLUNGE WITH CARE:** When placing battered vegetables into the oil, lower them gently and as close to the oil as possible to prevent splattering. Tongs or tweezers make this safe and easy.
- **SKIM THE BATTER DRIPPINGS:** In between batches, use a spider to scoop out stray bits of batter floating in the oil. Otherwise, they'll burn and impart a bitter flavor to your food.
- **TRANSFER FRIED VEGETABLES TO A WIRE RACK SET OVER A BAKING SHEET:** This allows the excess oil to drip away, keeping your vegetables crisp and dry. It works far better than draining on paper towels.

pomodori verdi fritti con l'uva

FRIED GREEN TOMATOES & GRAPES

Serves 4 as a side dish

- ¼ cup/30 g all-purpose flour
- Fine sea salt and freshly ground black pepper
- 4 green tomatoes
- ½ cup/120 ml high-heat vegetable oil, such as sunflower or peanut
- 3 garlic cloves, 2 unpeeled and 1 peeled and sliced
- ¼ cup/60 ml extra-virgin olive oil
- Red pepper flakes
- 1 small bunch of grapes (about 7 ounces/200 g), halved and seeded
- Handful of fresh basil leaves, torn if too big
- Handful of fresh mint leaves, torn if too big
- 2 tablespoons pine nuts, lightly toasted

This dish is a celebration of ingenuity, first crafted during that brief window when tomatoes on the vine lacked the sunlight to ripen them and farmers found themselves with baskets of green tomatoes and plump juicy grapes on hand at the same time. The combination of fried green tomatoes and grapes is brilliant.

The ingredient list is short, but each item plays a key role: Panfried green tomatoes are meaty and tangy, grapes bring delicate sweetness, garlic and herbs provide aromatic depth, and chile offers a gentle warmth. Serve this as a side dish alongside pork chops, grilled fish, or fresh mozzarella.

Place the flour on a plate and season with ½ teaspoon salt and a few grinds of pepper.

Cut the tomatoes crosswise into thick slices, then dredge them in the seasoned flour, coating evenly. Set aside.

Line a plate with paper towels and keep near the stove. Warm the vegetable oil in a large sauté pan over medium heat.

As the oil warms, add the unpeeled garlic cloves to infuse the oil with flavor. When the garlic starts to release its aroma, working in batches to avoid overcrowding, fry the tomato slices until golden, 3 to 5 minutes per side. Transfer the fried tomatoes to the paper towels to drain. Discard the garlic and carefully wipe the pan clean with paper towels.

Heat the olive oil in the same pan over medium heat. Add a big pinch of pepper flakes and the sliced garlic and cook until the garlic is lightly golden, about 3 minutes.

Add the tomatoes, halved grapes, basil and mint leaves, and toasted pine nuts. Toss gently to combine, then cook until the grapes begin to soften and collapse slightly, about 5 minutes.

Taste and adjust the seasoning with salt if needed. Serve immediately or keep warm until ready to eat.

VARIATION

Transform this dish into a satisfying main course by tossing the fried green tomatoes and grapes into beaten eggs to create a luscious frittata.

involtini di melanzane grigliate al pomodoro

GRILLED EGGPLANT ROLLS WITH TOMATO SAUCE

Makes 12; serves 4 as a main course

FOR THE EGGPLANT

- 2 large eggplants (about 15 ounces/425 g each)
- Fine sea salt
- Extra-virgin olive oil

FOR THE TOMATO SAUCE

- 3 tablespoons extra-virgin olive oil
- 1 garlic clove, minced
- 2 cups/500 g tomato passata
- 1 teaspoon fine sea salt
- Handful of basil leaves

FOR THE INVOLTINI

- 8 ounces/225 g scamorza, provolone, or mozzarella cheese, cut into 12 pieces
- 2 tablespoons grated Parmigiano Reggiano cheese

Grilled eggplant captures the taste of an Italian summer. I always keep a stash in the fridge, drizzled with olive oil; alongside roasted peppers (see page 33), it can become the building block to a satisfying meal. With a bit more effort, you can turn grilled eggplant into meatless roll-ups filled with scamorza, provolone, or mozzarella and nestled in a garlicky tomato sauce. Bring the pan of bubbling involtini right to the table, accompanied by a basket of crusty bread.

PREPARE THE EGGPLANT: Rinse the eggplants, trim them, and slice them lengthwise into slabs ⅓ inch/8 mm thick. Select the 6 largest slices from each eggplant, as they will be easier to roll up (see Notes).

Set a colander over a bowl, then layer the eggplant slices in the colander, sprinkling salt between the layers. Set them aside for 30 minutes. Salting the eggplants not only draws out their bitter water but also seasons them and makes grilling easier by reducing their moisture.

After 30 minutes, when a brownish liquid has gathered at the bottom of the bowl, gently squeeze the eggplants to remove excess liquid and pat them dry with paper towels.

Warm a large grill pan over medium heat and keep a plate ready nearby. Lightly brush both sides of the eggplant slices with olive oil.

When you pass your hand over the pan and you can feel the heat radiating, start grilling the eggplant slices in batches, without overcrowding the pan. Grill them until golden brown, glistening, and lightly charred in spots, 2 to 3 minutes per side. Transfer the grilled eggplant to the plate and repeat with the remaining slices.

MAKE THE TOMATO SAUCE: Place the olive oil and garlic in a large skillet and cook over low heat until fragrant, about 2 minutes. Stir in the tomato passata, salt, and basil leaves, cover, and simmer, stirring occasionally, over low heat until the tomato sauce is glossy and thick, about 20 minutes. Remove from the heat, season to taste, and set aside.

-recipe continues-

MAKE THE EGGPLANT INVOLTINI: Arrange an eggplant slice on a cutting board and place a piece of cheese at the bottom edge. Roll the eggplant tightly around the cheese and secure it with a toothpick. Repeat with the remaining eggplant slices.

Reheat the tomato sauce and place the eggplant involtini in the skillet, spooning some sauce over each roll. Cook the involtini over medium heat, covered, until the scamorza starts oozing from the sides, 5 to 6 minutes. Sprinkle with the grated Parmigiano Reggiano cheese and serve immediately.

Keep leftover involtini in the fridge for a couple of days and reheat them thoroughly in the tomato sauce before serving.

NOTES:

- Not every slice from the eggplants will be large enough to make into a roll-up. You can grill the smaller slices and serve them as an appetizer or snack, or use them in the Summer Vegetable Gratin (page 186).
- The grilled eggplant slices can be prepared in advance and stored in an airtight container in the fridge for a couple of days, as can the tomato sauce.

L'orto di Annas' garden

caponata di melanzane

EGGPLANT CAPONATA

Makes about 4 cups/900 g; serves 8 to 10 as an appetizer

- 3 medium eggplants (about 2¼ pounds/1 kg total), cut into ½-inch/13 mm cubes
- Fine sea salt
- 4 celery stalks, sliced
- ¼ cup/60 ml extra-virgin olive oil
- 1 small or ½ medium red onion, thinly sliced
- 1¼ cups/300 g tomato passata
- 1 cup/150 g Castelvetrano olives, pitted and roughly chopped
- 2 tablespoons brined or salt-packed capers, thoroughly rinsed
- ¼ cup/60 ml red wine vinegar, plus more to taste
- 1 tablespoon sugar, plus more to taste
- 3 tablespoons pine nuts, toasted
- 4¼ cups/1 L high-heat vegetable oil, such as sunflower or peanut

Sicilian caponata is a celebration of summer's bounty, a dish where humble ingredients such as eggplants, tomatoes, celery, and olives are transformed into a rich, sweet-and-sour delicacy. Traditionally made when gardens overflow with plump eggplants and sun-ripened tomatoes, caponata is deeply rooted in Sicily's culinary heritage and remains a beloved dish among locals and visitors alike.

Caponata can be served as a crowd-pleasing appetizer, a flavorful side, a bold topping for pasta, or spooned over toasted bread for a simple yet satisfying lunch, paired with fresh mozzarella. It also improves with time, as the flavors meld, so make it ahead and know that it will taste even better the next day.

Arrange the eggplants on a large tray and sprinkle with salt. Let sit for 30 minutes.

Bring a medium pot of water to a boil over high heat. Line a baking sheet with parchment paper.

Add the celery to the boiling water and blanch for 4 minutes. Use a slotted spoon to transfer it to the lined pan to drain.

Pour the olive oil into a large skillet, add the onion and blanched celery, season with a generous pinch of salt, and cook over medium heat until the onion gets soft and translucent, about 8 minutes.

Add the tomato passata, olives, and capers and cook over medium-low heat until the sauce is thick and glistens with oil, about 10 minutes.

Pour in the vinegar and sugar, stir thoroughly, and cook until the pungent smell of vinegar softens, about 3 minutes. Now taste: The sauce should be well balanced, with a pleasant sweet-and-sour taste. Adjust the seasoning with more sugar, vinegar, or salt, if needed. Add the toasted pine nuts and set aside.

Before frying the eggplants, blot them with paper towels to remove all the moisture.

Line a baking sheet with paper towels and keep near the stove. Pour the vegetable oil into a medium, deep pot and set it over medium-high heat. When the oil registers 350°F/175°C on a deep-frying thermometer, or when the handle of a wooden spoon dipped in the oil is immediately surrounded by tiny bubbles, you can start frying the eggplants.

Working in batches to avoid overcrowding, fry the eggplants until golden brown and soft, 5 to 8 minutes. Transfer them with a slotted spoon to the prepared baking sheet. Allow the oil to return to temperature between batches.

Transfer all the fried eggplant to the skillet with the tomato sauce, reheat, and simmer for 5 minutes, gently stirring the eggplants into the sauce while trying not to mash them. Transfer to a large bowl and let cool.

Serve at room temperature or cold. Eggplant caponata is even better the next day. Any leftovers can be kept in an airtight container in the fridge for up to 3 days.

VARIATION:

Artichoke Caponata

When eggplants are not available, make caponata with artichokes. Use 8 artichokes; if fresh artichokes are unavailable, substitute with 12 ounces/340 g frozen artichoke quarters. Thaw them overnight in the fridge.

Trim the fresh artichokes and cut them into 8 to 12 wedges, depending on their size. In a large pan, cook the artichokes with ¼ cup/60 ml extra-virgin olive oil and a crushed garlic clove until soft, about 15 minutes. Then add them to the prepared tomato sauce as in the recipe.

triangolini di pasta fillo con caponata di melanzane

PHYLLO POCKETS WITH EGGPLANT CAPONATA

Makes 16 caponata pockets

- 1 large egg, beaten
- 2 tablespoons whole milk
- 1 tablespoon extra-virgin olive oil
- 8 phyllo pastry sheets (13-by-18-inch/33 by 45 cm), thawed if frozen
- 1 recipe Eggplant Caponata (page 143)
- 2 tablespoons sesame seeds
- ¼ cup/80 g mild honey, like acacia
- 4 teaspoons 'nduja

Over the centuries, Sicily has been shaped by a rich tapestry of cultural influences—from the Greeks to the Arabs to the Normans and Spaniards—each leaving an indelible mark on its cuisine. These layered traditions are what make Sicilian food so vibrant and unique.

So it only makes sense to take caponata, one of Sicily's most beloved dishes, and wrap it in delicate golden phyllo pastry, a nod to the island's deep Greek and Middle Eastern ties. The result? Crisp, flaky pockets that crackle with every bite, giving way to the rich sweet-and-sour filling inside. Don't skip the honey and 'nduja dipping sauce.

Preheat the oven to 400°F/200°C. Line a baking sheet with parchment paper.

Mix together the egg, milk, and olive oil in a small bowl.

Open the phyllo pastry sheets, arrange them on a clean surface, and cover them with a damp tea towel to prevent them from drying up and breaking.

Take 2 sheets and keep the rest covered. Place one sheet on top of the other and brush them with the egg mixture. Starting from the long side, cut the phyllo sheets with a chef's knife or kitchen scissors into 4 equal strips.

Place about ¼ cup/60 g of caponata at one end of a phyllo strip. Starting with the end of the strip with the filling, fold one corner of the phyllo over the filling to form a triangle. Continue folding the strip in triangles, like you would fold a flag, until you end up with a triangular stuffed pastry. (See photos on page 146.)

Transfer the caponata triangle to the lined baking sheet and brush the sides, top, and bottom with the egg mixture.

Continue with the remaining strips. You should end up with 16 caponata pockets.

Sprinkle the pockets with the sesame seeds and transfer the baking sheet to the hot oven. Bake for 15 to 20 minutes, until the triangles are crisp and golden brown.

Remove the pockets from the oven and let them cool on the pan.

Meanwhile, in a small bowl, stir together the honey and 'nduja.

Arrange the caponata triangles on a serving platter and bring them to the table with the bowl of 'nduja honey for everyone to drizzle on top.

Leftover caponata triangles can be kept in the fridge for 2 days. Reheat them in a hot oven until crisp.

1
2
3
4

frittelle di cavolfiore

CAULIFLOWER & OLIVE FRITTERS

Makes about 35; serves 10 to 12 as an appetizer

FOR THE DOUGH

2¼ cups/300 g bread flour

1 cup plus 2 tablespoons/205 g semolina flour

½ teaspoon/1.5 g active dry yeast or instant yeast

1¾ cups plus 2 tablespoons/450 ml lukewarm water

2 teaspoons fine sea salt

2 tablespoons extra-virgin olive oil

FOR THE FRITTERS

Fine sea salt

1 pound 5 ounces/600 g cauliflower (1 small head), leaves removed

¼ cup/60 ml distilled white vinegar

⅓ cup/60 g Castelvetrano, Taggiasca, or Kalamata olives, pitted and roughly chopped

3 tablespoons brined or salt-packed capers, rinsed

4¼ cups/1 L high-heat vegetable oil, such as sunflower or peanut

Vegetable fritters can be light and airy, as in the fritto misto (Fried Vegetable Platter, page 133), or more doughy and dense, like these frittelle di cavolfiore. Salty from the capers and olives, yet delicate and creamy thanks to the cauliflower florets, fritters are an irresistible treat. This versatile recipe works with almost any vegetable: Try peppers and olives, zucchini and zucchini flowers. Anchovies or cubes of cheese make for excellent additions, too.

THE DAY BEFORE, MAKE THE DOUGH: Combine the bread flour, semolina flour, and yeast in a large bowl. Add all but 1 tablespoon of the warm water and mix with a wooden spoon until the dough comes together. It will be very sticky, soft, and not homogeneous. Cover with a damp towel and let rest for 20 minutes.

Add the salt and the remaining 1 tablespoon warm water and mix by squeezing the dough between your hands. The dough will become less sticky and more elastic, but it will still be soft like batter.

Pour the olive oil around the edges of the dough. Using wet hands, perform the stretch-and-fold technique: Pick up one edge of the dough, stretch it gently upward, and fold it over the top. Give the bowl a quarter-turn and repeat until you have completed four folds. Repeat this process three more times at 20-minute intervals over the next hour. The dough should become soft, elastic, and velvety. (See photos 1 and 2 on page 150.)

Cover the bowl with plastic wrap and let the dough rise at room temperature until doubled in size, 12 to 18 hours. (Alternatively, refrigerate for 22 to 24 hours and bring it back to room temperature before use.) The dough should be soft, wobbly, and lacy. (See photo 3 on page 150.)

PREPARE THE FRITTERS: Bring a large pot of water to a rolling boil and salt it generously. While the water heats, break the cauliflower into tiny florets. For larger pieces, halve, quarter, or chop them as needed—they should be small enough to blend seamlessly with the dough and form evenly shaped fritters. Rinse thoroughly and set aside.

Once the water boils, add the vinegar and plunge the cauliflower florets into the pot. Cook until barely tender, about 5 minutes. Drain, rinse the cauliflower under cold water, and let cool completely.

(The florets can be prepared 1 to 2 days ahead. Store them in an airtight container in the fridge until ready to use.)

Fold the cauliflower florets, olives, and capers into the risen dough with a spatula. If this gets tricky, use your hands to gently knead and squeeze them into the dough. (See photo 4 on page 150.)

Set a wire rack on a baking sheet or line a plate with parchment paper and keep near the stove. Pour the vegetable oil into a large, deep pan or Dutch oven and warm over medium-high heat. Preheat the oven to 210°F/100°C.

When a deep-frying thermometer registers 350°F/175°C or when the handle of a wooden spoon dipped into the oil is surrounded by tiny bubbles, the oil is ready for frying.

Working in batches to avoid overcrowding, drop spoonfuls of the dough into the hot oil. Aim for fritters no larger than a tablespoon, as they will puff up while frying. Fry, turning occasionally, until the fritters are puffed and golden, with nuggets of cauliflower a deep golden brown, 8 to 10 minutes. Use a slotted spoon to transfer the fritters to the wire rack or lined plate, and transfer them to the oven to keep warm. Allow the oil to return to temperature between batches.

Transfer the fritters to a serving platter and enjoy immediately, while still warm and crisp.

NOTE: Keep in mind that making this recipe requires some patience: The dough needs a long, slow rise to develop its delicate texture, so start a day ahead. Once it's ready, though, the fritters fry up in minutes.

1
2
3
4

radicchio tardivo grigliato con salsa verde e purè di fagioli

GRILLED RADICCHIO WITH GREEN SAUCE & CREAMY BEAN PUREE

Serves 4 to 6 as a main course

FOR THE SALSA VERDE

1 slice stale country bread (about 2 ounces/60 g), crust removed

¼ cup/60 ml white wine vinegar

1 large bunch of fresh parsley, stalks removed (about 1½ ounces/40 g)

2 tablespoons brined or salt-packed capers, rinsed thoroughly

1 garlic clove, peeled but whole

1 large hard-boiled egg, finely chopped

1 cup/240 ml extra-virgin olive oil

Fine sea salt and freshly ground black pepper

FOR THE BEAN PUREE

3 cups/700 g cooked cannellini beans (see Notes) or two 15.5-ounce/439 g cans cannellini, drained and rinsed

1 garlic clove, peeled

Grated zest and juice of 1 lemon, preferably organic

¼ cup/60 ml extra-virgin olive oil

2 teaspoons fine sea salt

-ingredients continue-

Radicchio Tardivo, with its creamy white stalks and curly, flaming purple leaves, is the most spectacular of the many Italian varieties of radicchio. Slightly bitter, it has a crisp, clean, wintery flavor, with a texture that is crunchy and juicy when raw and satisfyingly meaty when cooked.

My favorite way to cook radicchio is on a scorching-hot grill pan until nicely charred. The smokiness enhances its meaty texture, making this not just a seasonal side dish but a protagonist of the winter table. This main-course rendition is served with a lemony bean puree and finished with a zippy salsa verde and toasted pine nuts.

MAKE THE SALSA VERDE: Break the stale bread into big chunks, place in a medium bowl, and add the vinegar and ¼ cup/60 ml water. Let stand for 10 minutes, then squeeze the bread to remove the excess vinegar and crumble into a food processor. Pour out the bowl of vinegar and water and set aside the empty bowl.

Add the parsley, capers, and garlic to the food processor and pulse until you have a coarse paste. Transfer the parsley paste to the reserved bowl and add the chopped hard-boiled egg. Pour in the olive oil and stir to combine, then season with salt and pepper. Let stand for at least 1 hour at room temperature before serving so the flavors can mingle. (You can make the sauce in advance. It will keep in an airtight container in the fridge for up to 4 days; stir well before serving.)

MAKE THE BEAN PUREE: In a food processor, combine the beans, garlic, lemon zest, lemon juice, olive oil, and salt. Process until you have a creamy, smooth puree, about 3 minutes, scraping down the sides of the bowl as needed. You might add up to ¼ cup/60 ml water (or bean cooking liquid; see Notes) to make it smoother if needed. Taste and adjust the seasoning. (You can make the bean puree in advance. It will keep in the fridge for up to 4 days; stir well before serving.)

-recipe continues-

FOR THE GRILLED RADICCHIO

4 heads radicchio Tardivo (see Notes), about 8 ounces/225 g each

TO SERVE

Fine sea salt

2 tablespoons pine nuts, toasted

GRILL THE RADICCHIO: Rinse the radicchio Tardivo heads under running water, then quarter them lengthwise.

Place a cast-iron griddle pan over medium heat and have a large plate nearby.

When the griddle is hot—it should sizzle and hiss when you toss a few drops of water in it—add the radicchio quarters. Working in batches, grill the radicchio on each side until wilted and nicely charred all over, then transfer it to the plate.

TO SERVE: Spoon the bean puree onto a large serving plate. Pile the radicchio on top and sprinkle it with salt. Drizzle the radicchio with half of the salsa verde and finish with the toasted pine nuts. Serve the radicchio immediately with more salsa verde on the side.

NOTES:

- If you cook your own beans, save ¼ cup/60 ml of the cooking liquid for the bean puree and use it instead of the water called for in the recipe.
- If radicchio Tardivo is difficult to find, substitute with Treviso precoce, Chioggia, or radicchio di Verona.

ITALIANS AND BITTER FLAVORS

IN ITALIAN CUISINE, BITTERNESS IS MORE THAN JUST A FLAVOR PROFILE; it is a cultural cornerstone, embraced in ways few other cuisines do. Italy's unique relationship with bitterness is not just about tolerance—it is a profound appreciation. According to Massimo Montanari, one of Italy's leading food historians, this cultural inclination stems from the country's historical reliance on vegetables. Bitter greens, either cultivated or foraged, have always been central to the peasant diet. Over time, these humble ingredients crossed into the kitchens of the upper classes, as the culinary habits of peasants and aristocrats were more interconnected than one might think. This shared tradition laid the foundation for a cuisine rich in vegetables, with bitterness taking a celebrated role.

Bitter flavors are the last to be acquired in the development of the human palate. As we grow, we discover that they can be intriguing, palatable, and even exciting. We might transition from indulging in milk chocolate bars to savoring the complexity of dark chocolate with a sprinkle of sea salt. We might crave a well-brewed coffee in the morning or a hoppy craft beer to wind down at the end of the day. Our palates refine over time, and we gladly enjoy the bitterness found in broccoli, Brussels sprouts, kale, dandelion greens, radicchio, artichokes, or grapefruit.

Consider the Italian appreciation for amaro, the bitter liqueur that often concludes a meal—Amaro Lucano or Amaro Averna, for example. In Italy, every region, every town, and sometimes even individual restaurants have their own house amaro. Not to mention the monasteries, which still produce some of Italy's most celebrated amari. Amaro serves as a key ingredient in an aperitivo, like Campari. And Italians created Cynar, a liqueur made from thirteen herbs and plants, including artichoke—the very symbol of bitterness. Even our soft drinks lean toward a marked bitter taste, like cedrata, aranciata amara, or chinotto, my personal favorite.

Italians understand that bitterness adds complexity and excitement to food. Amaro may be the iconic example, but the principle applies throughout our cuisine. From artichokes to the endless varieties of radicchio, arugula to dandelion greens, bitter vegetables are staples on Italian tables.

Bitterness pairs especially well with umami and fat. Parmigiano Reggiano cheese, when shaved copiously on top, elevates the clean bitterness of thinly sliced raw artichokes or of a peppery, feathery salad of radicchio and arugula. Creamy blue cheese like Gorgonzola pairs beautifully with radicchio, whether stirred into risotto or tossed with pasta or gnocchi (see page 114). Nuts work just as well, so don't skimp on walnuts and hazelnuts when preparing a kale salad (see page 25).

Extra-virgin olive oil, with its naturally bitter undertones, is often the fat of choice for Italians. Blanched or boiled bitter greens, such as turnip tops, escarole, or kale, take on incredible flavor when sautéed in garlicky, chile-infused olive oil. Winter, with its CSA boxes brimming with bitter greens, is the perfect season to embrace bitterness the Italian way, with the help of your finest extra-virgin olive oil. Bitter flavors will make the winter days more bearable, and definitely more interesting.

BAKED & ROASTED

Caramelizing the natural sugars in vegetables and creating deep, complex flavors is easy when you use your oven. Roasting brings out earthy sweetness, while baking transforms vegetables into hearty casseroles and savory pies.

parmigiana bianca di zucchine

WHITE ZUCCHINI PARMIGIANA

Serves 6 to 8

- 5 medium zucchini (about 2¼ pounds/1 kg total)
- Fine sea salt
- 3 medium potatoes (about 1½ pounds/700 g total)
- Extra-virgin olive oil
- 1 pound/450 g fresh mozzarella, cut into bite-size pieces
- 8 ounces/225 g scamorza or provolone, thinly sliced
- 3 large eggs, lightly beaten
- 3½ ounces/100 g Parmigiano Reggiano cheese, finely grated (about 1¾ cups firmly packed)
- Fresh basil leaves

Even though I could eat eggplant parmigiana even on the hottest summer day, there are moments when I crave something lighter and fresher. That's when I turn to this white zucchini and potato parmigiana. Layered with mozzarella, scamorza, Parmigiano, and a generous handful of basil leaves, it's a dish that captures the essence of an Italian summer.

Rinse the zucchini and slice them lengthwise into slices ¼ inch/6 mm thick. Set a colander over a bowl and layer the zucchini slices inside, sprinkling each layer with salt. Let them rest for 30 minutes. The salt will draw out excess moisture, making the cooking process easier.

Peel and slice the potatoes into rounds ⅛ inch/3 mm thick. Rinse them and place them in a medium pot. Cover with cold water and add 1 teaspoon salt. Bring the water to a boil, cook for 1 minute, then turn off the heat. Drain the potatoes, rinse them under cold water, and set them aside.

After 30 minutes, gently press the zucchini to remove any remaining moisture and pat them dry with paper towels.

Heat a cast-iron griddle over medium heat until hot (you should feel the heat radiating when you hold your hand above the surface). Working in batches so the zucchini doesn't overlap, grill the slices until golden brown with charred spots, 2 to 3 minutes per side. Transfer to a plate.

Preheat the oven to 350°F/175°C.

Drizzle a 9-by-13-inch/23 by 33 cm baking dish with olive oil. Start by layering half the potato slices on the bottom. Top with one-quarter of the mozzarella and scamorza, spoon over about one-quarter of the beaten eggs, and sprinkle with one-quarter of the grated Parmigiano. Scatter fresh basil leaves on top.

Next, layer half of the zucchini slices, followed by one-quarter of the mozzarella and scamorza, one-quarter of the beaten eggs, and one-quarter of the grated Parmigiano. Scatter more basil leaves.

Repeat both layers again: potatoes or zucchini, cheeses, eggs, Parmigiano, and basil. Finish with a generous sprinkling of Parmigiano, basil leaves, and a drizzle of olive oil. Transfer to the hot oven.

Bake until golden brown on top, 35 to 40 minutes.

Serve the parmigiana warm, or let it cool and reheat it later—it'll be even tastier. Store leftovers in the fridge for 2 days and reheat well before serving.

pomodori arrosto

ROASTED TOMATOES

Makes about 4 cups/950 ml

2 pounds/900 g mixed tomatoes, such as Fiorentini ribbed tomatoes, Roma, San Marzano, or beefsteak

4 small shallots (about 100 g total), peeled and halved

A few basil leaves

⅓ cup/80 ml extra-virgin olive oil

1 teaspoon fine sea salt

Freshly ground black pepper

Summer tomatoes are magnificent when slow-roasted with shallots, basil, and a generous glug of extra-virgin olive oil. The gentle, prolonged heat coaxes out their sticky sweetness, concentrating the essence of the season. This method, though, also works wonders on lackluster, out-of-season tomatoes, whether picked too early or nearing the end of their prime, nudging them to reveal their best flavor.

Preheat the oven to 350°F/175°C.

Rinse the tomatoes, cut them in half, then arrange them cut side up in a 9-by-13-inch/23 by 33 cm baking dish or roasting pan. Scatter the shallots among the tomatoes along with a few basil leaves. Drizzle everything generously with the olive oil and season with the salt and pepper to taste. Transfer the pan to the oven.

Roast the tomatoes until they're soft, slightly caramelized, and just starting to collapse, about 1½ hours. Keep an eye on them—different tomato varieties and sizes may roast at slightly different times.

Use the tomatoes immediately in your favorite recipe, or keep them in the fridge in an airtight container for up to 5 days. They can also be frozen for up to 6 months.

A QUICK RECIPE TO MAKE WITH ROASTED TOMATOES:

ROASTED TOMATO SOUP

With freshly roasted tomatoes, you can prepare a comforting soup for 2 to 3 people, about three ½-cup/ 120 ml servings. In a blender, blend the roasted tomatoes with the shallots, oil, and all the juices from the pan until smooth and creamy. Adjust the seasoning to taste with salt and pepper. If the soup is too thick, add 1 cup/240 ml hot water, vegetable stock, or tomato water (see Notes, page 221) and simmer gently over medium heat. If it's too thin, continue simmering until the soup reaches your desired consistency.

Meanwhile, cut 2 slices of bread into cubes and cook them in a pan with a drizzle of olive oil until crisp and golden brown.

Serve the soup hot, topped with a handful of crispy croutons and a spoonful of cold ricotta or crumbled goat cheese—the contrast is delightful. Finish with a few turns of freshly ground black pepper and a final drizzle of high-quality extra-virgin olive oil.

orzotto ai pomodori arrosto

ROASTED TOMATO ORZOTTO

Serves 4 as a main course, 6 as a first course

- 1½ cups/300 g pearled barley
- 4 cups/950 ml Roasted Tomatoes (page 162), with pan juices, thoroughly reheated
- Fine sea salt
- 3 tablespoons/45 g unsalted butter
- 2 small shallots (about 50 g total), finely minced
- ½ cup/120 ml dry white wine
- 4 cups/960 ml hot vegetable stock (see page 124) or tomato water (see Notes, page 221)
- ½ ounce/14 g Parmigiano Reggiano cheese, finely grated (about ¼ cup firmly packed)
- 8 ounces/225 g stracciatella or burrata, torn into small pieces
- Freshly ground black pepper

An orzotto is just a risotto made with orzo, the Italian word for barley. (Do not confuse the grain orzo with the small barley-shaped pasta of the same name.) Pearled barley's nutty al dente texture magnificently absorbs the flavor of any ingredient you pair it with. It's easy to make, filling, and nutritious.

Barley takes a bit longer to cook than rice, and the cooking time can vary depending on the brand you use. Pearled barley, which has some of the bran removed, is the best option for quicker cooking. Because of this, the amount of stock you'll need is approximate. The key is to keep stirring and adding liquid until you achieve the texture you like: tender but still a bit chewy and al dente. Unlike risotto, barley doesn't release as much starch, so the orzotto tends to be less creamy. However, in this recipe, the roasted tomato puree and the addition of stracciatella create a luscious, rich texture that more than makes up for it.

Soak the barley in a bowl of cold water for about 2 hours.

In a food processor, blend the roasted tomatoes with the pan juices until creamy. Adjust the seasoning with salt. Set aside.

In a large saucepan, melt the butter over low heat and add the shallots. Season with a generous pinch of salt so they release their moisture and cook without burning. Stir and cook until translucent and soft but not browned, about 5 minutes.

Drain the barley and add it to the shallots. Increase the heat to medium-low and toast for 2 to 3 minutes, until shiny. Pour the wine over the barley and let it evaporate, stirring with a wooden spoon until absorbed and the alcohol smell is gone, 3 to 5 minutes.

Add a ladleful of the hot stock and cook, stirring often. Ladle in additional cups of stock anytime the barley looks dry.

After about 15 minutes, when the barley is halfway through the cooking, stir in the pureed tomatoes and keep cooking, adding more stock until the barley is creamy, soft, and still slightly al dente, about 20 minutes. You might not need all the stock; timing may vary depending on the type of barley you use.

Remove the pan from the heat, add the grated Parmigiano and half of the stracciatella, and stir the barley with a wooden spoon until well combined with the cheese and very creamy. Taste and season with salt.

Spoon the orzotto into serving bowls, top each portion with the remaining stracciatella, add a few turns of pepper, and serve immediately.

pizzette capricciosa di zucca e melanzane

SQUASH & EGGPLANT PIZZETTE CAPRICCIOSA

Serves 4 to 6 as a main course

¼ cup/60 ml extra-virgin olive oil

1 teaspoon fine sea salt

12 slices eggplant, ¼ inch/6 mm thick, cut crosswise from the thickest side of the eggplant

12 slices butternut squash, ¼ inch/6 mm thick, cut from the top side, peeled and without seeds

FOR THE TOMATO SAUCE

One 14-ounce/400 g can whole peeled tomatoes

2 tablespoons extra-virgin olive oil

1 teaspoon dried oregano

½ teaspoon fine sea salt

FOR THE TOPPINGS

5 white button mushrooms

Fine sea salt

½ tablespoon extra-virgin olive oil

2 ounces/56 g prosciutto cotto or cooked ham, cut into thin slices

4 oil-packed baby artichokes, homemade (see page 217) or store-bought, quartered

2 tablespoons Taggiasca or Kalamata olives, pitted and cut into rounds

Handful of fresh basil leaves

When you crave pizza but don't have the time to make the dough, try these pizzette. Slices of eggplant or butternut squash are piled high with crushed peeled tomatoes, mozzarella, and a mix of toppings inspired by the classic pizza capricciosa: olives, artichokes, prosciutto cotto, and fresh basil. After a short blast in the oven, you have something that, while not exactly pizza, captures its essence beautifully.

It's a quick, scrumptious, and fun solution for a midweek dinner, entirely gluten-free, and proof that a little improvisation often leads to the best and most rewarding meals.

Arrange one rack in the lower third of the oven and a second rack in the center and preheat the oven to 400°F/200°C. Line two baking sheets with parchment paper.

In a small bowl, whisk together the olive oil, salt, and 1 tablespoon water until well emulsified. Generously brush both sides of the eggplant and squash slices with the oil, ensuring they're well coated. Arrange them in a single layer on the lined pans.

Transfer the vegetables to the hot oven and roast until they take on a light golden color and become tender, 12 to 15 minutes.

WHILE THE VEGETABLES ROAST, MAKE THE TOMATO SAUCE: Using your hands, crush the peeled tomatoes into a medium bowl. (Peeled tomatoes work better than passata, because they add a nicer texture to the pizzette, and are generally less watery.) Drizzle with the olive oil, season with the dried oregano and salt, and stir to combine.

Once the vegetables are golden, remove them from the oven and spoon a tablespoon of the fresh tomato sauce over each slice.

Return the pans to the oven and bake for an additional 10 to 12 minutes, rotating the pans and switching the position of the pans on the racks halfway through to ensure even roasting.

WHILE THE PIZZETTE BAKE, PREPARE THE TOPPINGS: Thinly slice the mushrooms and sauté them for a minute in a dry nonstick pan. After they have released some of their moisture and started to cook down, sprinkle them with a generous pinch of salt, drizzle with the olive oil, and cook until golden and slightly crisp, 2 to 3 more minutes. Set them aside.

- 1 teaspoon dried oregano
- 8 ounces/225 g fresh mozzarella cheese, diced

Once the tomato sauce is bubbling and the vegetables are crisping up, remove the pizzette from the oven. Top each slice with pieces of prosciutto cotto, quartered baby artichokes, olives, and cooked mushrooms. Scatter with basil leaves, sprinkle with oregano, and top each slice with mozzarella.

Return the baking sheets to the hot oven and bake until the mozzarella has melted and turned golden in spots, about 7 minutes.

Serve the pizzette immediately. Leftover pizzette can be stored in an airtight container in the fridge for up to 3 days and briefly reheated in a hot oven before serving.

la parmigiana di melanzane di nonna

MY GRANDMA'S EGGPLANT PARMIGIANA

Serves 6 to 8

FOR THE EGGPLANT

4 large eggplants

Fine sea salt

¼ cup/30 g all-purpose flour

2 cups/480 ml high-heat vegetable oil, such as sunflower or peanut

FOR THE TOMATO SAUCE

2 tablespoons extra-virgin olive oil

1 garlic clove, smashed and peeled

2 cups/500 g tomato passata

A few basil leaves

Fine sea salt

FOR ASSEMBLY

3 large eggs, lightly beaten

½ pound/225 g fresh mozzarella, cut into bite-size pieces

3½ ounces/100 g Parmigiano Reggiano cheese, finely grated (about 1¾ cups firmly packed)

Extra-virgin olive oil, for drizzling

Summer isn't officially over until I make a few trays of eggplant parmigiana to freeze for the colder months. This might not be the traditional recipe for eggplant parmigiana—though, really, who decides what is truly traditional?—but it's the one my nonna has been making since I was a child. Layers of fried eggplant, rich tomato passata, mozzarella, and Parmigiano, all brought together with beaten eggs. The addition of eggs is unusual, but they are what make my nonna's parmigiana so unique—rich, dense, easy to cut, and delicious.

PREPARE THE EGGPLANT: Slice the eggplants lengthwise into slices ¼ inch/6 mm thick. Set a colander over a bowl and arrange the eggplant in layers sprinkled with sea salt. After 30 minutes, when a brownish liquid has gathered at the bottom of the bowl, gently squeeze the eggplant to remove excess water and pat it dry with paper towels.

Pour the flour onto a shallow plate and dust the eggplant slices with flour. Set aside.

Line a plate with paper towels and keep near the stove. Heat the vegetable oil in a large saucepan over medium-high heat to 350°F/175°C on a deep-frying thermometer—or when a wooden spoon handle dipped into the oil is surrounded by tiny bubbles.

Working in batches to avoid overcrowding, fry the eggplant until golden and crisp, about 5 minutes per side. Transfer to the paper towels to drain.

MAKE THE TOMATO SAUCE: Warm the olive oil in a saucepan over medium heat. Add the garlic and cook until golden. Pour in the tomato passata, ½ cup/120 ml water, and a few basil leaves. Season with a pinch of salt and simmer for about 10 minutes, stirring occasionally, until thickened and flavorful.

ASSEMBLE THE DISH: Preheat the oven to 350°F/175°C. Spread a few tablespoons of the tomato sauce on the bottom of a 9-by-13-inch/ 23 by 33 cm baking dish. Layer the dish beginning with the fried eggplant and following with the tomato sauce, beaten eggs, mozzarella pieces, and grated Parmigiano. Repeat the layers until all ingredients are used, finishing with a generous topping of tomato sauce, mozzarella, Parmigiano, and a drizzle of olive oil. Transfer to the hot oven.

Bake until golden brown on top, 35 to 40 minutes.

Serve the parmigiana warm, or let it cool and reheat it later—it'll be even tastier. Store leftovers in the fridge for 2 days and reheat well before serving.

VARIATION:

Butternut Squash Parmigiana

When autumn arrives, I turn to squash for my parmigiana. Substitute the eggplant with 2 pounds/900 g butternut squash, peeled, seeded, and thinly sliced. Preheat the oven to 400°F/200°C and lightly dust each slice with flour. Grease two baking sheets with olive oil and arrange the squash slices in a single layer. Drizzle with extra-virgin olive oil, sprinkle with salt, and bake until golden and crisp, about 35 minutes. Then continue with the recipe as written.

zucca al forno

ROASTED SQUASH

Makes about 4 cups/900 g

- 1 medium Mantovana squash (see Note), about 4½ pounds/2 kg, halved lengthwise and seeded
- 1 red onion, peeled and halved
- 2 garlic cloves, unpeeled
- 2 fresh rosemary sprigs
- A dozen fresh sage leaves
- ¼ cup/60 ml extra-virgin olive oil
- 1 teaspoon fine sea salt
- A few grinds of black pepper

My favorite squash for roasting is Mantovana, with its dark, green-gray edible peel and orange pulp, compact and sweet. It grows in the north of Italy around Mantua, in the region of Lombardy, but it is known all over the country. Roast it halved, with herbs and aromatics nestled into its cavities to infuse their flavor into its pulp. Use the roasted squash to make risotto, gnocchi, soups, tortelli, and quick pasta sauces, or mix it with mashed potatoes for a comforting side dish (see page 174).

Preheat the oven to 400°F/200°C. Line a baking sheet with parchment paper.

Place the squash on the lined pan, cut side up. Nestle the halved onion, garlic cloves, rosemary, and sage leaves into the squash cavities. Season with the olive oil, salt, and pepper and rub the surface of the squash with your fingers to distribute the seasonings.

Roast until the squash is golden, almost caramelized on the edges, and with a pulp so soft that it can be scooped out with a spoon, about 1 hour (see Note).

When it's cool enough to handle, use a spoon to scoop out the flesh (discard the skin and the aromatics). Use the squash immediately in your favorite recipe or keep it in the fridge in an airtight container for up to 5 days. It can also be frozen for up to 6 months.

NOTE: This recipe works with any small-to-medium squash: delicata, acorn, butternut squash, kabocha, and red kuri squash, with its distinct chestnut flavor. The roasting time may vary depending on the size and texture of the squash, so check the squash after about 40 minutes. It will be ready when you are able to easily scoop out the roasted pulp with a spoon.

A QUICK RECIPE TO MAKE WITH ROASTED SQUASH:

ROASTED SQUASH SOUP

In a blender, combine 3 cups/700 g roasted squash pulp, half the roasted onion, the roasted garlic removed from its skin, and 2 cups/470 ml vegetable or chicken stock. Blend until smooth, then adjust the seasoning with salt and pepper. Serve topped with toasted sliced almonds, browned pancetta bits, or a dollop of fresh ricotta and a grating of lemon zest.

gattò di patate e zucca

SAVORY POTATO & SQUASH PIE

Serves 6 as a main course

- 2¼ pounds/1 kg baking potatoes, such as russet (about 3 medium)
- Softened butter, for the pie pan
- 4 tablespoons/20 g coarse breadcrumbs, preferably homemade (see page 84)
- 2 cups/450 g Roasted Squash (page 173)
- 6 tablespoons/85 g unsalted butter, plus more to dot the pie
- 2 large eggs
- 3½ ounces/100 g Parmigiano Reggiano cheese, finely grated (about 1¾ cups firmly packed)
- 1½ teaspoons fine sea salt
- Freshly ground black pepper
- 8 ounces/225 g smoked scamorza or provolone cheese, grated (about 1½ cups)
- 4 ounces/115 g prosciutto cotto or cooked ham, diced (about ¾ cup)

This savory potato pie makes a terrific dinner. It was a staple in my family when I was a child, always delivering its comforting embrace after a long day. When I began cooking for my own family, I carried a bunch of my mum's recipes with me, tweaking them with my own preferences, exploring new flavors, and creating personal variations. This potato and squash pie was born from that experimentation, combining my favorite autumn ingredient with a dish that heralds the arrival of colder days. The result is a creamy, comforting pie, oozing with melted cheese and crowned with golden, crispy breadcrumbs. Serve this pie alongside a sharp radicchio salad.

Choose potatoes that are roughly the same size, so that they can cook evenly in the boiling water. Arrange the potatoes in a pot where they can comfortably sit in one layer. Add water to cover and bring to a boil, covered, over medium heat. Reduce to a simmer and cook the potatoes until you can easily pierce them with a knife, 40 to 45 minutes. Drain and run the potatoes under cold water, removing the skins.

Preheat the oven to 350°F/175°C. Grease a 9-inch/23 cm deep-dish pie pan, round baking dish, or ovenproof pot with butter and coat with 2 tablespoons of the breadcrumbs.

Mash the potatoes by pressing through a food mill or a potato ricer into a large bowl. Mixing while the potatoes are still hot, add the roasted squash, butter, eggs, Parmigiano, salt, and several grinds of pepper. Use a fork to make a creamy, smooth texture. Fold the smoked scamorza and diced prosciutto into the potato and squash mash.

Spoon the mash into the prepared baking dish, then smooth the surface with a spatula and sprinkle the pie with the remaining 2 tablespoons breadcrumbs and dot it with slivers of butter.

Transfer to the hot oven and bake until golden and crisp, 40 to 45 minutes.

Serve warm. Keep the leftovers in the fridge in an airtight container for up to 4 days. Reheat in a hot oven or the microwave before serving.

LEFT: Radicchio & Potato Strudel
RIGHT: Savory Potato & Squash Pie

strudel di radicchio e patate

RADICCHIO & POTATO STRUDEL

Serves 6 to 8 as a main course

FOR THE STRUDEL DOUGH

2 cups/250 g all-purpose flour, plus more for dusting

3 tablespoons vegetable oil

1 teaspoon white wine vinegar

¼ teaspoon fine sea salt

FOR THE FILLING

1 pound/450 g yellow waxy potatoes (about 2 medium)

¼ cup/60 ml extra-virgin olive oil

1 fresh rosemary sprig

½ medium red onion, thinly sliced

1 ¼ pounds/567 g radicchio (about 1 large or 2 medium heads), shredded

1 cup (3 ½ ounces/100 g) walnuts, chopped

Fine sea salt and freshly ground black pepper

5 ounces/142 g Asiago cheese, diced

4 ounces/115 g Gorgonzola cheese, cut into small chunks

FOR ASSEMBLY

Extra-virgin olive oil, for drizzling

1 tablespoon poppy seeds

What could rival the charm of an apple strudel, laced with cinnamon and melted butter? A savory version, wrapped in a quick, versatile dough and filled with your favorite combination of vegetables and cheese. This radicchio and potato strudel makes a striking vegetarian main dish, perfect for Thanksgiving or winter holidays.

Making strudel from scratch is a hands-on process that requires time, space, and patience. The dough needs to rest for a few hours or overnight, allowing the gluten to relax so it can be stretched until almost transparent. You'll need a large work surface and a tablecloth to help you roll it out. While one person can stretch the dough, having a second set of hands makes the process easier—especially for beginners.

MAKE THE STRUDEL DOUGH: Do this the day before, or at least a couple of hours in advance. Dump the flour onto a work surface, make a well in the center, and add the vegetable oil, vinegar, and salt. Begin mixing with a fork, gradually incorporating ½ cup plus 2 teaspoons/120 ml water until fully combined. Knead the dough until soft, silky, and shiny on the surface, about 10 minutes. (Alternatively, use a stand mixer with the dough hook on low speed for about 10 minutes, then finish with 2 minutes of hand-kneading.) Wrap the dough in plastic wrap and let it rest at room temperature for about 1 hour. If making it the night before, refrigerate the dough and bring it back to room temperature before using.

MAKE THE FILLING: Peel and dice the potatoes, adding them to a large bowl of cold water as you work. Rinse and drain them in a colander to remove excess starch, then pat them dry with a clean kitchen towel.

Heat the olive oil in a large heavy-bottomed pan over medium heat. Add the rosemary sprig to infuse the oil. After a couple of minutes, add the onion and potatoes, tossing well. Cook over medium heat, stirring frequently, until the potatoes are soft and golden, 15 to 20 minutes.

Add the radicchio in batches, letting some of it wilt before adding more. Stir it into the potatoes and cook over medium heat, stirring frequently, until wilted, dark purple, and reduced by half, about 10 minutes.

Add the walnuts, taste, and adjust the seasoning with salt and pepper. If the filling seems too bitter, remember the cheese will tone it down. Set aside to cool.

Once cooled, add the Asiago and Gorgonzola, tossing gently to combine. (The filling can be made a day ahead; let cool, cover, and refrigerate until ready to use.)

ASSEMBLE THE STRUDEL: Preheat the oven to 400°F/200°C. Line a baking sheet with parchment paper.

Spread a clean tablecloth on your work surface and sprinkle it lightly with flour. With a lightly floured rolling pin, roll out the dough into a disk ⅜ inch/1 cm thick. Drape the dough over the backs of your hands and gently stretch it by turning and pulling from the edges.

Place the dough flat on the floured tablecloth. Working from the center, slide your hands, backs up, under the dough and carefully stretch it outward in all directions until paper-thin and nearly transparent, about 28 by 40 inches/70 by 100 cm. Don't worry about small tears—just patch them and keep going; they won't matter once rolled. Drizzle with 2 tablespoons olive oil.

Starting from a short side, spoon the filling onto half of the dough, leaving a ¾-inch/2 cm border. Fold in the sides and roll up the dough using the tablecloth to help. Seal the ends, trim excess dough, and transfer seam side down onto the lined pan. If needed, form a U shape.

Brush the strudel with 1 tablespoon olive oil and sprinkle the surface with the poppy seeds.

Transfer the strudel to the hot oven and bake until golden brown and crisp, about 30 minutes.

Let it cool for at least 10 minutes before slicing with a serrated knife for clean slices. Serve warm or at room temperature.

Keep the remaining strudel in the fridge and reheat thoroughly in a hot oven before serving.

VARIATION:

Potato & Squash Strudel

Use 1 pound/450 g potatoes and swap in 1 pound/450 g winter squash for the radicchio. Dice them and cook them with 1 leek and a handful of sage leaves as in the recipe, omitting onion and rosemary. Add 10 ounces/284 g cubed Fontina cheese instead of Asiago and Gorgonzola and ½ cup (1½ ounces/43 g) sliced almonds in place of walnuts. Cooking and baking methods are the same as in the recipe.

gnocchi alla romana con la zucca

SQUASH SEMOLINA GNOCCHI

Serves 6 as a main course

- 2 cups/450 g Roasted Squash (page 173)
- 3¼ cups/750 ml whole milk
- Freshly grated nutmeg
- Fine sea salt
- 1½ cups/250 g semolina flour
- 7 tablespoons/100 g unsalted butter, at room temperature, cut into cubes
- 2 large egg yolks
- 3½ ounces/100 g Parmigiano Reggiano cheese, finely grated (about 1¾ cups firmly packed)
- Neutral oil, for the pan
- Softened butter, for the baking dish
- Handful of fresh sage leaves

Gnocchi alla romana—despite what their name suggests—hail not from Rome but from northern Italy. Made with fine semolina flour, milk, and butter, these gnocchi contain no potatoes at all. In this version, roasted squash adds a seasonal twist, lending a gorgeous orange hue and a naturally sweet, delicate flavor.

These gnocchi are a true lifesaver when hosting family and friends. You can prepare them ahead of time and simply bake them just before serving. They're also perfect for busy weeknights when you're craving something comforting but don't have time to cook from scratch. Just pop them in the oven, and in no time, you'll have a golden, bubbling tray of gnocchi alla romana.

In a medium nonstick skillet, mash the roasted squash and set over medium heat for about 5 minutes, mashing it constantly with a spatula against the bottom and sides of the pan until it becomes smooth and thickens and the liquid evaporates.

Combine the milk, nutmeg to taste, and 2 teaspoons salt in a large saucepan. Set the saucepan over medium heat and, when the milk starts to steam, sprinkle the semolina in a slow and steady stream, stirring constantly to avoid lumps.

If needed, remove the saucepan from the heat and blend the mixture with an immersion blender to remove any remaining lumps. Add the squash puree and mix it in until smooth and pale orange, without visible streaks of squash puree.

Return the saucepan to medium-low heat and stir constantly with a wooden spoon until the mixture thickens into a smooth, dense mashed potato–like consistency and begins to pull away from the sides of the saucepan, 7 to 10 minutes. It should become challenging to stir it because it will be thick and heavy. Remove from the heat.

Add half of the cubed butter and stir it in with a spatula until it has completely melted. Add the egg yolks and half of the grated Parmigiano. Stir until the gnocchi dough is smooth and well combined, then taste and add more salt if needed.

Line a baking sheet with parchment paper and lightly grease the paper with oil. Scoop the squash and semolina polenta onto the parchment paper, and using a greased spatula, spread it into a layer ½ inch/13 mm thick. Smooth the surface with the spatula. Grease another sheet of parchment paper with oil and place it over the gnocchi dough, greased side down. Refrigerate for at least 2 hours, or overnight, to allow it to firm up.

Preheat the oven to 400°F/200°C. Butter a 12-inch/30 cm round baking dish.

Dip a 2½-inch/6.5 cm round cookie cutter in water to prevent it from sticking to the gnocchi dough. Cut out rounds from the chilled semolina dough, dipping the cutter in water again every two or three gnocchi. Press back together the dough scraps to cut more rounds. Aim for 22 to 24 rounds total.

Arrange the gnocchi slices in the buttered baking dish, slightly overlapping them in concentric circles to create an attractive pattern. Dot with the remaining cubed butter, sprinkle generously with the rest of the Parmigiano, and scatter fresh sage leaves over the top.

Transfer the gnocchi to the hot oven and bake until golden and crisp on the edges, 25 to 30 minutes.

Serve them immediately, straight from the oven.

If you have leftovers, store them in an airtight container in the fridge for up to 2 days. Reheat in a hot oven or microwave before serving to bring back their delicious melt-in-your-mouth texture.

VARIATION

For a comforting twist, coat the gnocchi with a generous blanket of béchamel sauce (see page 181). Sprinkle them with Parmigiano before baking until golden brown and bubbling on the edges.

NOTES:

- The gnocchi can be frozen either before or after baking, making them a great make-ahead option. If freezing them before baking, arrange the gnocchi in the baking dish, dot them with butter, and sprinkle with Parmigiano. Cover tightly and freeze. When ready to bake, transfer directly from the freezer to a 400°F/200°C oven and bake until golden and crisp on the edges, 35 to 40 minutes.
- If freezing them after baking, let them cool completely, then place the entire dish in the freezer. When ready for serving, transfer them straight from the freezer to a hot oven and warm at 350° to 375°F/175° to 190°C for 15 to 20 minutes, until heated through and slightly crisp on the edges.

lasagne con zucca e funghi

SQUASH & MUSHROOM LASAGNA

Serves 8 as a first course

FOR THE ROASTED SQUASH

1¾ pounds/800 g butternut, Mantovana, delicata, or acorn squash, peeled and seeded

2 fresh sage sprigs, leaves picked

¼ cup/60 ml extra-virgin olive oil

Fine sea salt

Freshly grated nutmeg

FOR THE BESCIAMELLA

7 tablespoons/100 g unsalted butter, cut into pieces

¾ cup plus 1 tablespoon/100 g all-purpose flour

4¼ cups/1 L whole milk

1 teaspoon fine sea salt

Freshly grated nutmeg

Freshly ground black pepper

FOR THE PORCINI

1 pound/450 g fresh porcini mushrooms (see Notes)

2 tablespoons extra-virgin olive oil

1 garlic clove, peeled but whole

5 fresh thyme sprigs, leaves picked

Fine sea salt

¼ cup/60 ml dry white wine

Freshly ground black pepper

-ingredients continue-

While the most traditional lasagna calls for besciamella sauce and a rich beef and pork ragù, lasagna is an endlessly adaptable canvas for seasonal vegetables and cheeses. Fall is all about squash and mushrooms. This combination shines in many forms, from a savory Potato and Squash Strudel (page 177) to Mushroom and Ricotta Stuffed Crepes (page 204), but it's especially satisfying when layered with béchamel, Taleggio, and Parmigiano, as in this lasagna.

ROAST THE SQUASH: Preheat the oven to 400°F/200°C.

Slice the squash into slices ⅛ inch/3 mm thick and arrange them on a baking sheet. Scatter the sage leaves on top. Drizzle with the olive oil and season with salt and nutmeg. Toss the squash to distribute the coating evenly. Arrange the slices so that they are just slightly overlapping.

Slide the baking sheet into the hot oven, and bake until the squash is cooked through, golden, and glistening with oil, 25 to 30 minutes. Set aside. (This can be done in advance and kept in the fridge for up to 2 days.)

MAKE THE BESCIAMELLA: Melt the butter in a saucepan over medium heat. When the butter is melted, add the flour and whisk for a few minutes until golden and toasted. Pour in the milk in a thin stream, whisking constantly to avoid lumps. Cook the besciamella, still stirring constantly, until thickened, 2 to 3 minutes; your whisk should leave visible trails in the sauce. Season with the salt, nutmeg, and pepper to taste. (You can prepare the besciamella in advance, let it cool, and keep it in an airtight container in the fridge for up to 2 days. Gently reheat it before using.)

COOK THE PORCINI: Brush the porcini to remove any dirt, then slice them and set aside.

In a large sauté pan, combine the olive oil, garlic, and thyme leaves and season with a pinch of salt. Cook over medium heat, stirring occasionally, until fragrant, about 2 minutes.

Add the porcini and cook for 5 more minutes, stirring often. Pour in the white wine, increase the heat to medium-high, and cook until almost completely evaporated, 5 to 6 minutes. Taste and adjust the seasoning with salt and pepper. Discard the garlic, then set aside. (The mushrooms can be prepared in advance and refrigerated for 2 days.)

-recipe continues-

FOR ASSEMBLY

- Softened butter, for the baking dish
- 1 pound/450 g lasagna sheets, store-bought or homemade (see Notes)
- 8 ounces/225 g Taleggio cheese, cubed (see Notes)
- 3 ounces/84 g Parmigiano Reggiano cheese, finely grated (about 1½ cups firmly packed)
- Handful of fresh sage leaves
- Extra-virgin olive oil, for drizzling

ASSEMBLE THE LASAGNA: Preheat the oven to 400°F/200°C. Generously butter a 9-by-13 inch/23 by 33 cm baking dish.

If using dried lasagna sheets, soak them in a large pot of hot tap water for 20 minutes, then drain them. Arrange all your ingredients nearby, including the warm besciamella, roasted squash, cooked porcini, and cheeses.

Begin with a layer of pasta sheets to cover the bottom of the dish completely: Trim the sheets as needed to fit the dish. Spoon a thin layer of besciamella over the pasta, spreading it evenly. Arrange a layer of roasted squash, followed by the sautéed porcini, and scatter a small handful of Taleggio cubes. Sprinkle with grated Parmigiano.

Repeat this layering process—pasta, besciamella, squash, mushrooms, Taleggio, and Parmigiano—until all the ingredients are used. Aim for five complete layers. Decorate the top with fresh sage leaves and drizzle with a little olive oil.

Slide the dish into the hot oven and bake until the top is golden brown and bubbling with cheese, about 45 minutes.

Let the lasagna rest for 10 minutes before serving warm. For an even more flavorful dish, allow it to cool completely, then refrigerate overnight. When ready for serving, cover the lasagna with aluminum foil and reheat it at 400°F/200°C for about 20 minutes, until heated through. Remove the foil for the last few minutes to restore the crisp, golden top.

VARIATIONS

In spring, layer fresh asparagus, peas, and fava beans, swapping the béchamel for something tangier like stracchino or stracciatella. In summer, try cherry tomatoes and mozzarella. When winter arrives, lean into the comforting bitterness of sautéed radicchio paired with crunchy walnuts and béchamel.

NOTES:

- If fresh porcini are difficult to come by, try a combination of cremini, chanterelle, oyster, shiitake, or portobello mushrooms plus 1 ounce/28 g dried porcini to enhance the mushroom flavor. Soak the dried porcini in water for about 30 minutes, then discard the water, squeeze them, chop them, and add them to the pan along with the other mushrooms.
- Use store-bought lasagna sheets or make your own (recipe follows). If using store-bought, either use fresh ones as is or soak dried sheets in hot tap water for 20 minutes to soften. Drain well before assembling.
- Taleggio is a cow's milk cheese produced in Val Taleggio, an alpine valley in Lombardy. Pungent in smell and rich in flavor, it melts beautifully in sauces, polenta, gratins, and savory pies. If you can't find Taleggio, substitute with Fontina or Brie.

FRESH LASAGNA SHEETS

Makes 1 pound/450 g

1½ cups plus 2 tablespoons/200 g tipo "00" flour or all-purpose flour, plus more for dusting

½ cup plus 1 tablespoon/100 g semolina flour

3 large eggs

Fine sea salt

1 teaspoon extra-virgin olive oil

Mound both flours on a clean work surface. Use the bottom of a bowl to press down in the center, creating a large, deep well—this will hold your wet ingredients. Crack the eggs into the well, add a pinch of salt and the olive oil, and begin stirring with a fork. Work slowly, starting from the center and gradually pulling in the flour from the edges. As the dough begins to form, it will come together in crumbly pieces. If the mixture feels too dry, add water a few drops at a time, up to 1 tablespoon, stirring gently until the dough comes together.

Once the dough is crumbly but cohesive, gather it with your hands, pressing and squeezing it into a ball. Begin kneading by hand, stretching and folding the dough on the work surface. Knead for about 10 minutes, until your hands and the surface are clean and the dough feels smooth, silky, and slightly elastic. (If using a stand mixer with the dough hook, knead for 5 minutes on low speed, then finish by hand for another 5 minutes to perfect the texture.)

Cover the dough with an overturned bowl or wrap it loosely in plastic wrap. Let it rest at room temperature for 30 minutes to relax the gluten and make it easier to roll out.

ROLL THE DOUGH BY HAND: Dust a baking sheet and your work surface with semolina flour. Divide the dough into 2 portions. Work with one portion at a time and keep the remaining dough covered so it won't dry out. Use a rolling pin to roll the dough into a paper-thin sheet of pasta.

ROLL THE DOUGH USING A PASTA MACHINE: Divide the dough into 8 equal portions. Lightly dust a work surface with semolina flour and slightly flatten one portion with a rolling pin. Keep the rest covered under a clean kitchen towel or a bowl. Set your pasta machine to the widest setting. Feed the dough through the rollers, then fold it into thirds, like a letter. Rotate so an open side faces the rollers and repeat. Do this three times to develop elasticity.

Begin rolling the dough thinner by narrowing the settings on the machine, one step at a time. Each time, feed the dough through the rollers while gently pulling it toward you to keep the sheet straight. Use one hand to receive the pasta sheet and the other to turn the crank. Continue until the sheet is as thin as desired. For lasagna sheets, this is usually the eighth setting on a Marcato or KitchenAid pasta machine.

Lay the rolled sheet on a floured surface and repeat with the rest. If using immediately, no need to cover the sheets. If not, keep them under a damp kitchen towel to prevent them from drying out.

verdure estive gratinate

SUMMER VEGETABLE GRATIN

Serves 6 to 8 as a side dish

- 1 medium eggplant
- 2 small sweet onions
- 3 medium Roma (plum) tomatoes
- 3 bell peppers, a mixture of red, yellow, and green
- ½ cup/ 120 ml extra-virgin olive oil
- Fine sea salt

FOR THE BREADCRUMBS

- 1½ cups/ 120 g coarse breadcrumbs, preferably homemade (see page 84)
- 3 garlic cloves, peeled
- 3 tablespoons brined or salt-packed capers, thoroughly rinsed
- 2 tablespoons dried oregano
- 1 tablespoon fresh thyme leaves
- Handful of fresh basil leaves
- 2 ounces/ 56 g Parmigiano Reggiano cheese or Pecorino Romano (or a mixture of both), finely grated (about 1 cup firmly packed)
- Fine sea salt
- ¼ cup/ 60 ml extra-virgin olive oil

My family has always loved hosting summer gatherings in the garden. One of our most beloved side dishes is a tray of gratin vegetables. We slice up whatever the garden is producing—eggplants, peppers, zucchini, onions, and even slightly unripe tomatoes—and arrange them on a large baking sheet. Once softened in the oven, the veg is scattered with breadcrumbs for a crisp, golden finish. Mix the breadcrumbs with your favorite fresh or dried herbs, sharp grated cheese, garlic, capers, olives, or even a touch of lemon zest.

Make more of this vegetable gratin than you think you'll need. It's just as delicious the next day, even at room temperature; you can build a meal around it, pairing the vegetables with a salad and some high-quality canned tuna. These vegetables also work magic in a sandwich with a thick slice of mozzarella.

Arrange one rack in the lower third of the oven and a second rack in the center and preheat the oven to 400°F/200°C.

Rinse the eggplant and cut it crosswise into slices ⅓ inch/8 mm thick. Do the same with the onions and tomatoes. Halve the peppers, seed them, and cut them into large strips.

Coat two baking sheets with some of the olive oil. Arrange the vegetables on the pans, slightly overlapping the slices, then brush them generously with the remaining olive oil. Sprinkle with salt.

Roast for 15 minutes, rotating the pans between racks halfway through for even cooking.

MEANWHILE, PREPARE THE BREADCRUMBS: In a food processor, combine the breadcrumbs, garlic, capers, oregano, thyme, and basil and process until finely chopped. Transfer to a bowl and stir in the grated cheese. Taste and adjust the seasoning with salt. Drizzle in the olive oil and ¼ cup/60 ml water. This helps retain moisture and prevents the breadcrumbs from drying out before the vegetables are fully cooked.

After 15 minutes, remove the vegetables from the oven and scatter the breadcrumb mixture evenly over top. Return the pans to the oven and bake for another 15 minutes, switching the position of the pans on the racks halfway through, until the vegetables are golden brown and the breadcrumbs are crisp. Serve immediately.

Leftover vegetables can be stored in the fridge for up to 3 days. Reheat briefly before serving.

STUFFED

A celebration of abundance and creativity, these recipes highlight the Italian tradition of either stuffing vegetables with flavorful mixtures of breadcrumbs, grains, cheeses, and herbs, or using vegetables themselves as fillings for pasta, crespelle, involtini, and cascioni. In both cases, vegetables are key in hearty, satisfying dishes that are the essence of home-cooked comfort.

peperoni ripieni di riso

RICE-STUFFED PEPPERS

Serves 6 as a first course, 3 as a main course

FOR THE RICE

¼ cup/60 ml extra-virgin olive oil

½ small red onion, minced

Fine sea salt

1 ⅓ cups/250 g Carnaroli or Arborio rice

About 2¾ cups/650 ml hot vegetable stock

1 ounce/28 g Parmigiano Reggiano cheese, finely grated (about ½ cup firmly packed)

FOR THE STUFFED PEPPERS

3 large bell peppers, red and yellow

2 Roma (plum) tomatoes, seeded and diced

¼ cup/30 g black olives, such as Taggiasca or Kalamata, pitted and sliced

6 ounces/170 g provolone cheese, diced

Fine sea salt

Extra-virgin olive oil, for brushing and drizzling

2 tablespoons coarse breadcrumbs, preferably homemade (see page 84)

Bell peppers are built to be stuffed, their shape a perfect receptacle for ground meat, mashed potatoes and sausages, canned tuna and breadcrumbs, some leftover pasta, and rice, or better yet risotto, as in this case. You'll bake the peppers until their skins become wrinkled and charred in spots, their slightly smoky and sweet aroma filling your kitchen.

COOK THE RICE: Heat the olive oil in a medium saucepan over low heat. Add the onion and a generous pinch of salt to help release its moisture, allowing it to soften without browning. Cook, stirring occasionally, until the onion is translucent and soft but not browned, about 5 minutes.

Add the rice, increase the heat to medium, and toast, stirring frequently, until the grains are pearly and slightly translucent, 5 to 6 minutes.

Pour in all the hot stock at once, reduce the heat to medium-low, and simmer, stirring occasionally, until the liquid is absorbed and the rice is cooked through and creamy, 18 to 20 minutes. The cooking time and the amount of stock needed may vary depending on the rice used.

Stir in the grated Parmigiano, mixing vigorously with a wooden spoon to create a creamy consistency. Taste and adjust the seasoning with salt. Transfer the rice to a medium bowl and let it cool slightly. The rice can be prepared a day ahead and kept in an airtight container in the fridge until the next day.

MEANWHILE, PREPARE THE PEPPERS: Bring a medium pot of water to a boil. Halve the bell peppers lengthwise, removing the stems and seeds. Plunge the pepper halves into the boiling water and cook until slightly softened but still holding their shape, 4 to 8 minutes. Remove the peppers from the boiling water and drain on paper towels.

Add the diced tomatoes, olives, and provolone to the cooled rice. Mix well with a spoon to incorporate all the ingredients, then taste and adjust the seasoning with salt.

Preheat the oven to 350°F/175°C.

Brush the pepper halves all over with olive oil, then spoon the rice filling into each one, pressing gently to compact it. Arrange the filled peppers on a baking sheet, sprinkle with the breadcrumbs, and drizzle generously with olive oil. If there's extra filling, transfer it to a small baking dish, sprinkle with additional breadcrumbs, drizzle with olive oil, and bake alongside the peppers.

Transfer the pan to the hot oven and bake until the peppers are cooked through and wrinkled and the rice is golden, 45 to 50 minutes. If desired, place them under the broiler for 5 minutes for a crisp, golden topping.

Let the peppers rest for 10 minutes before serving. Keep any leftovers in the fridge for up to 2 days. Reheat thoroughly in a hot oven or microwave before serving.

cipolle ripiene

POTATO-STUFFED ONIONS

Serves 4 as a main course, 8 as an appetizer

- 4 medium yellow onions (about 7 ounces/200 g each)
- ¼ cup/60 ml extra-virgin olive oil, plus more for greasing and drizzling
- 6 fresh thyme sprigs, leaves picked
- 2 fresh marjoram sprigs, leaves picked
- Fine sea salt
- 1 pound/450 g starchy potatoes, such as russet, peeled, boiled, and riced (or mashed), about 2 cups packed
- 2 ounces/56 g Parmigiano Reggiano cheese, finely grated (about 1 cup firmly packed)
- 2 ounces/56 g mortadella, minced
- Freshly ground black pepper
- 2 large eggs, lightly beaten
- Homemade Breadcrumbs (page 84)

Potatoes, much like breadcrumbs, have a way of elevating other humble ingredients. In these Ligurian-inspired stuffed onion shells, boiled and mashed potatoes transform simple seasonal produce into the centerpiece for the table.

Bring a large pot of water to a boil.

Meanwhile, peel and trim the onions, taking care to keep their shape intact.

Plunge the onions into the boiling water and cook until you can easily pierce them with a knife, about 30 minutes. Drain and let them cool slightly.

Preheat the oven to 400°F/200°C. Lightly grease a baking sheet with olive oil.

Halve the onions lengthwise and, using a spoon, carefully scoop out their centers, leaving a sturdy shell made of 3 layers. Finely mince the scooped-out onion cores.

Warm the olive oil in a large skillet over low heat. Add the minced onions, thyme and marjoram leaves, and a generous pinch of salt. Cook gently, stirring occasionally, until the onions are soft, creamy, and golden, about 40 minutes.

Transfer the cooked onions to a large bowl. Add the riced potatoes, grated Parmigiano, and mortadella. Stir thoroughly to combine. Taste and adjust the seasoning with salt and pepper. Stir in the beaten eggs until the filling is smooth and cohesive.

Arrange the onion shells on the prepared baking sheet. Generously stuff each shell with the potato filling, shaping it into a mound. Sprinkle the tops with breadcrumbs and drizzle generously with olive oil.

Transfer the baking sheet to the hot oven and bake until the tops are golden brown and crisp, 25 to 30 minutes.

Serve the onions warm or at room temperature.

Store any leftovers in an airtight container in the fridge for up to 4 days. Reheat gently in a low oven or microwave before serving.

VARIATIONS

Affordable, ingenious, and endlessly adaptable, the same filling can be used to stuff hollowed-out zucchini, tomatoes, mushrooms, eggplants, and peppers.

LEFT: Potato-Stuffed Onions
RIGHT: Bread-Stuffed Mushrooms

funghi ripieni

BREAD-STUFFED MUSHROOMS

Serves 4 as a main course, 8 as an appetizer

- ⅔ packed cup (about ⅓ ounce/10 g) dried porcini or shiitake mushrooms
- 12 large cremini mushrooms (about 1 pound/450 g total), each the size of a golf ball
- 5¼ ounces/150 g day-old country bread, cut into chunks, or 1 large thick slice of a sourdough boule
- 3 tablespoons extra-virgin olive oil, plus more as needed
- 1 garlic clove, minced
- 1 teaspoon finely chopped fresh parsley
- Fine sea salt
- Red pepper flakes (optional)
- ¼ cup/25 g walnuts, finely chopped
- 2 ounces/56 g Pecorino Romano cheese, finely grated (about 1 cup firmly packed)
- 1 teaspoon finely chopped fresh mint
- Freshly ground black pepper
- 2 large eggs, lightly beaten
- Homemade Breadcrumbs (page 84)
- 4 small or 2 medium potatoes (about 14 ounces/400 g total), peeled and cut into thin wedges

In my kitchen, every crumb of bread has a purpose. I make it a point to meticulously gather leftover corners and day-old slices to transform into homemade breadcrumbs (see page 84). This isn't just about respecting ingredients or embracing the principles of cucina povera—the Italian resourceful, no-waste approach to cooking. It's because breadcrumbs are highly versatile and have the power to transform a dish. Toasted, they add an irresistible crunch to pasta or vegetables. Breadcrumbs also work exceptionally well as a stuffing, either for chicken, beef braciola, or seasonal vegetables. Here they absorb flavor, add texture, and deliciously enhance these mushrooms.

Place the dried porcini mushrooms in a medium bowl and cover them with hot water. Be generous with the water, as you'll need it to soak the bread, too. Let the mushrooms steep for about 30 minutes, allowing the water to extract their earthy, aromatic notes.

While the porcini are steeping, clean the cremini mushrooms by brushing off any dirt. Carefully detach the stems from the caps, setting the caps aside. Finely chop the stems and set them aside, too.

Once the porcini have steeped, scoop them out of the water, squeezing out any excess liquid back into the bowl, and finely chop them. Reserve the soaking water and set the chopped porcini aside.

Add the bread to the porcini soaking liquid, pressing it down to submerge fully. If there is not enough water in the bowl to fully submerge the bread, add more hot water to the bowl. Let the bread soak for 5 minutes or until soft, which might take a little longer. Drain and discard the porcini soaking water, then squeeze out as much water as possible from the bread. Crumble the softened bread into a large bowl.

Warm the olive oil in a medium skillet over low heat. Add the garlic, parsley, and a generous pinch of salt. Add pepper flakes to taste, if desired, for a gentle warmth in the filling. Cook, stirring often, until the garlic is fragrant and barely golden, about 5 minutes.

Add the chopped cremini stems, chopped porcini, and walnuts. Stir to coat in the oil and cook, stirring frequently, until browned, about 10 minutes.

Transfer the cooked mushrooms and walnuts to the bowl with the crumbled bread. Add the Pecorino Romano and mint. Mix thoroughly with your hands, mashing as you go. Taste and adjust the seasoning with salt and pepper. Finally, stir in the beaten eggs until the filling is cohesive and smooth.

Preheat the oven to 400°F/200°C. Lightly grease a 10-inch/26 cm round baking pan with olive oil.

Arrange the cremini caps in the prepared baking pan. Generously stuff each cap with the bread filling, shaping it into a rounded mound. Sprinkle the tops with breadcrumbs.

Arrange the potato wedges around the mushrooms in the pan. Season the potatoes with salt and drizzle everything generously with olive oil.

Transfer the baking pan to the hot oven and bake until the mushroom tops are golden brown and crisp and the potatoes are tender, 25 to 30 minutes.

Serve the stuffed mushrooms warm or at room temperature, accompanied by the roasted potatoes.

Store any leftovers in an airtight container in the fridge for up to 4 days. Reheat gently in a low oven or microwave before serving.

cappellacci al cacao con zucca, noci e castagne

COCOA CAPPELLACCI STUFFED WITH ROASTED SQUASH, WALNUTS & CHESTNUTS

Makes 60 to 70 cappellacci; serves 6 to 8

FOR THE PASTA DOUGH

2½ cups/313 g tipo "00" flour or all-purpose flour

1 tablespoon unsweetened cocoa powder, preferably Dutch-process

3 large eggs

1 teaspoon extra-virgin olive oil

Pinch of fine sea salt

FOR THE FILLING

1 teaspoon extra-virgin olive oil

1 cup/100 g walnuts

2 cups/450 g Roasted Squash (page 173)

1 roasted garlic clove (from the Roasted Squash recipe; see page 173)

3½ ounces/100 g peeled cooked chestnuts or store-bought steamed chestnuts, crumbled

1¾ ounces/50 g Parmigiano Reggiano cheese, finely grated (about 1 scant cup firmly packed)

6 fresh sage leaves, finely chopped

¼ teaspoon freshly grated nutmeg

Fine sea salt and freshly ground black pepper

-ingredients continue-

This unusual fresh pasta dough is made with the addition of unsweetened cocoa powder; it has only a hint of cocoa, so do not expect chocolate-flavored pasta. It marries beautifully with savory fillings and dressings like sausages and pecorino but also with butternut squash. Using Dutch-process cocoa powder will give a deeper color and flavor.

MAKE THE PASTA DOUGH: Place the "00" flour and cocoa powder onto a clean work surface and shape them into a mound. Use the bottom of a bowl to press down in the center, creating a large, deep well—this will hold your wet ingredients. Crack the eggs into the well, add the olive oil and salt, and begin stirring with a fork. Work slowly, starting from the center and gradually pulling in the flour from the edges. As the dough begins to form, it will come together in crumbly pieces. If the mixture feels too dry—cocoa powder tends to absorb moisture—add water a few drops at a time, up to 2 tablespoons, stirring gently until the dough comes together.

Once the dough is crumbly but cohesive, gather it with your hands, pressing and squeezing it into a ball. Begin kneading by hand, stretching and folding the dough on the work surface. Knead for about 10 minutes, until the dough feels smooth, silky, and slightly elastic. (If using a stand mixer with the dough hook, knead for 5 minutes on low speed, then finish by hand for another 5 minutes to perfect the texture.)

Cover the dough with an overturned bowl or wrap it loosely in plastic wrap. Let it rest at room temperature for 30 minutes to relax the gluten and make it easier to roll out.

WHILE THE DOUGH IS RESTING, MAKE THE FILLING: Warm the olive oil in a skillet over medium heat. Add the walnuts and toast them gently, shaking the pan often to prevent burning, until they turn a rich golden brown and release their nutty aroma, about 10 minutes. Transfer the toasted walnuts to a plate to cool. When the walnuts are completely cool, grind them into a coarse powder using a blender or food processor.

-recipe continues-

FOR THE CAPPELLACCI

Semolina flour, for rolling

Fine sea salt

11 tablespoons/ 150 g unsalted butter, cut into pieces

20 fresh sage leaves

Grated Parmigiano Reggiano cheese, for serving

Place the roasted squash in a large bowl. Squeeze the soft, caramelized garlic clove out of its skin and add to the squash. Stir in the ground walnuts, crumbled chestnuts, Parmigiano, chopped sage, and nutmeg. Using a fork, mash the filling thoroughly until it becomes thick and homogeneous. Taste the filling and adjust the seasoning with salt and a few turns of pepper.

MAKE THE CAPPELLACCI: Dust a baking sheet and a work surface with semolina flour. Divide the dough into 2 equal portions if rolling by hand, or 8 equal portions if using a pasta machine. Work with one portion at a time and keep the remaining dough covered with a clean kitchen towel so it won't dry out.

If rolling by hand, use a rolling pin to roll the dough into a paper-thin sheet of pasta.

If you're using a pasta machine, slightly flatten one piece of dough with a rolling pin. Set your pasta machine to the widest setting. Feed the dough through the rollers, then fold the sheet into thirds, like a letter. Turn the dough so one of the open sides faces the rollers and feed it through the machine again. Repeat this folding and rolling process three times to build elasticity.

Begin rolling the dough thinner by narrowing the settings on the machine, one step at a time. Each time, feed the dough through the rollers while gently pulling it toward you to keep the sheet straight. Use one hand to receive the pasta sheet and the other to turn the crank. Continue until the sheet is as thin as desired. For cappellacci, this is usually the seventh setting on a Marcato or KitchenAid pasta machine.

Lay the rolled pasta sheet on your floured work surface. Using a 3-inch/7.5 cm round cutter, cut the sheet into rounds. Gather any scraps and place them back under the kitchen towel for reuse.

Place 1½ teaspoons of filling in the center of each round. Fold the round in half to form a crescent, and press the edges firmly with your fingers to seal. If the edges don't seal properly, a light brush of water will help them stick together.

Gently press the center of the crescent to create a slight indent in the belly of the cappellaccio. Bring the two outer corners together at the bottom, overlapping them slightly, and press firmly to seal.

Transfer the formed cappellacci to the prepared baking sheet. Cover them with a clean, dry kitchen towel as you work to prevent them from drying out.

Repeat the rolling and shaping process with the remaining dough and filling. Gather the scraps, lightly knead them into a smooth ball, and roll them out as described above. (Freeze the cappellacci now if you don't want to cook them immediately; see Note.)

Bring a large pot of water to a rolling boil and salt it generously.

Melt the butter in a large skillet over medium-low heat. Add the sage leaves and fry gently until the butter turns golden brown, releasing its nutty aroma, and the sage becomes crisp. Remove the skillet from the heat and set it aside.

When the water comes to a boil, add the cappellacci in batches to avoid overcrowding and cook until the pasta is tender and cooked through, 3 to 5 minutes. Use a spider or slotted spoon to lift the cappellacci from the pot, letting the excess water drip off.

Transfer the cappellacci directly into the skillet with the browned butter and sage. Toss gently to coat each one in the sauce, being careful not to break them.

Serve immediately, topped generously with grated Parmigiano. Enjoy this dish at its best—hot and freshly tossed!

VARIATIONS

When it comes to the filling for this unique pasta, let the seasons be your guide. In autumn, roasted squash is my favorite choice, a nod to the traditional cappellacci alla zucca from Romagna. Sometimes, I enrich it with mushrooms, chestnuts, walnuts, or the sweet, delicate crunch of amaretti, creating a dish that feels perfectly in tune with the changing leaves and cooler days.

NOTE: If you do not want to cook the cappellacci immediately, you can freeze them by placing them in a single layer on a baking sheet generously dusted with semolina flour. Once frozen, transfer to a zip-top bag and store for up to 3 months. Alternatively, store them in the fridge for a few hours.

conchiglioni ripieni al forno

RICOTTA & CAULIFLOWER STUFFED SHELLS

Serves 6 as a first course

Fine sea salt

1 small Romanesco cauliflower (about 1 pound 5 ounces/600 g) or white cauliflower, leaves and hard stem removed

2 tablespoons extra-virgin olive oil, plus more for drizzling

1 garlic clove, smashed and peeled

Freshly ground black pepper

15 to 16 ounces/425 to 450 g ricotta (about 2 cups)

3½ ounces/100 g Gorgonzola cheese, cut into small pieces

3½ ounces/100 g provolone, coarsely grated

2 ounces/56 g Pecorino Romano cheese, finely grated (about 1 cup firmly packed)

16 ounces/450 g conchiglioni or jumbo shells (45 to 50 shells)

Softened butter, for the baking dish

Handful of fresh sage leaves

2 tablespoons coarse breadcrumbs, preferably homemade (see page 84) or panko

2 tablespoons/30 g unsalted butter

When you're short on time or simply not in the mood to make stuffed fresh pasta from scratch, turn to the glorious oversized pasta shapes in the package: conchiglioni (jumbo shells), lumaconi, or paccheri. Their concave shapes and generous size are perfect vessels for all kinds of fillings, from a rich, hearty meat ragù to lighter combinations like ricotta and seasonal vegetables. Once stuffed, these jumbo shells transform in the oven, turning golden brown, bubbling, and crisp. It's a dish that feels indulgent and festive, comes together effortlessly, and is perfect for cozy family dinners or gatherings with friends.

Bring a large pot of water to a rolling boil and salt it generously. Meanwhile, break the cauliflower into small florets, halving or quartering the larger ones, and rinse well. Once the water boils, add the florets and cook until the largest pieces can be easily pierced with a knife, 8 to 12 minutes. Remove with a slotted spoon and let cool in a bowl. (The florets can be prepared 1 to 2 days ahead and stored in an airtight container in the fridge.) Reserve the cooking water for the pasta.

Warm the olive oil in a large pan over medium-low heat. Add the garlic and cook until golden and fragrant, about 2 minutes. Add the florets, toss to coat, and cook, stirring often, until soft and creamy, 10 to 15 minutes. Season with salt and pepper, discard the garlic, and set aside.

In a large bowl, mix the ricotta, cooked cauliflower, Gorgonzola, provolone, and Pecorino Romano. Stir until the cheeses are fully incorporated into the cauliflower. Taste and adjust the seasoning. (The filling can be made a day ahead and stored in the fridge in an airtight container.)

Bring the reserved pot of water back to a rolling boil. Cook the pasta until al dente according to the package directions. Drain, rinse briefly under cold water, and toss with olive oil to prevent sticking.

Preheat the oven to 400°F/200°C. Grease a large round or oval baking dish generously with butter.

Spread a little filling over the bottom of the dish. Stuff each shell and arrange them snugly. Top with some sage leaves and breadcrumbs, and dot with small pieces of butter.

Bake until golden brown, crisp, and bubbling slightly around the edges, about 30 minutes. Serve immediately.

Leftovers keep in the fridge for a couple of days; reheat thoroughly before serving.

crespelle ai funghi

MUSHROOM & RICOTTA STUFFED CREPES

Serves 4

FOR THE CRESPELLE

- 3 large eggs
- ¼ cup/30 g all-purpose flour
- 2 tablespoons/15 g rye flour
- Fine sea salt
- 1¼ cups/300 ml whole milk
- Extra-virgin olive oil, for the pan

FOR THE FILLING

- 1 pound (450 to 500 g) fresh porcini (see Note)
- ¼ cup/60 ml extra-virgin olive oil
- 1 garlic clove, minced
- 3 fresh thyme sprigs, leaves picked and finely chopped
- 2 fresh marjoram or oregano sprigs, leaves picked and finely chopped
- Fine sea salt
- ½ cup/120 ml dry white wine
- Freshly ground black pepper
- 1¼ cups (10 ounces/283 g) fresh whole-milk cow or sheep ricotta
- 1 ounce/28 g Parmigiano Reggiano cheese, finely grated (about ½ cup firmly packed)
- 5 ounces/142 g Fontina cheese, diced (about 1 cup)

Commonly prepared with spinach and blanketed in besciamella and tomato sauce, crepes, known as crespelle in Italy, are easy to make. Use ricotta as the backbone of your filling, then add mushrooms, asparagus, artichokes, roasted squash, or just a bunch of fresh herbs along with some grated pecorino.

MAKE THE CRESPELLE: In a large bowl, whisk the eggs with both flours and a pinch of salt. Make sure there are no flour lumps. Pour the milk in a thin stream and whisk to incorporate until you get a smooth, runny batter. Cover the bowl with plastic wrap and put it in the fridge for about 1 hour. Don't skip the resting time: It makes the batter slightly thicker, giving the flour time to hydrate completely and allowing any air bubbles trapped in the batter to float to the top and dissipate, thus resulting in crepes with a better texture and taste.

Remove the batter from the fridge and whisk it briefly.

Warm an 8-inch/20 cm nonstick skillet over medium heat and place a plate nearby. Soak a paper towel in olive oil and brush it on the hot pan.

Pour a scant ladle—about ¼ cup/60 ml—batter into the hot pan, then swirl the pan to cover it with a thin layer. Cook for about 2 minutes until the crepe has golden brown, crisp, lacy edges, then flip it with a spatula and cook it on the other side for about 30 seconds.

Move the first crepe onto the plate and repeat with the remaining batter. Stack the crespelle on top of each other as they are ready. You should get 8 crespelle. Set the finished crespelle aside. (You can also prepare them in advance and keep them covered with plastic wrap in the fridge for a couple of days.)

MAKE THE FILLING: Brush the porcini to remove any dirt, then slice them and set them aside.

In a large sauté pan, combine the olive oil, garlic, thyme, and marjoram and season with a pinch of salt. Cook over medium heat, stirring occasionally, until fragrant, about 2 minutes.

Add the porcini and cook for 5 more minutes, stirring often. Pour in the white wine, increase the heat to medium-high, and cook until almost completely evaporated, 5 to 6 minutes. Taste and adjust the seasoning with salt and pepper.

FOR THE BESCIAMELLA

2 tablespoons/30 g butter

¼ cup/30 g all-purpose flour

1 ¼ cups/300 ml whole milk

Fine sea salt

½ teaspoon freshly grated nutmeg

FOR ASSEMBLY

Softened butter, for the baking dish

Extra-virgin olive oil, for drizzling

Scoop out a handful of cooked porcini and set aside to use when finishing the dish. Transfer the remaining porcini to a bowl. Add the ricotta, Parmigiano, and about two-thirds of the diced Fontina, then gently fold all the ingredients into the ricotta. Taste and season with salt and pepper. Set aside.

MAKE THE BESCIAMELLA: Melt the butter in a medium saucepan over medium heat. When the butter is melted, add the flour and whisk for a few minutes until golden and toasted. Pour in the milk in a thin stream, whisking constantly to avoid lumps. Cook the besciamella for a few minutes, stirring constantly, until thickened; your whisk should leave visible trails in the sauce. Add salt to taste and the nutmeg. (You can prepare the besciamella in advance, let it cool, and keep it in the fridge for up to 2 days. Gently reheat it before using, and add a splash of milk to loosen it up if needed.)

ASSEMBLE THE CRESPELLE: Preheat the oven to 400°F/200°C. Grease a 10-inch/25 cm round ceramic baking dish with butter.

Spread each crepe with ½ cup/about 90 g of the porcini and ricotta filling. Fold them as you would a handkerchief—first in half, then in half again. (See photos on page 206.) Arrange the crespelle, overlapping them slightly in the prepared baking dish.

Drizzle the crespelle with the besciamella sauce, then top with the reserved porcini and the remaining Fontina. Drizzle with extra-virgin olive oil.

Transfer the crespelle to the hot oven and bake for about 30 minutes, until golden brown and bubbling on the sides.

Eat the crespelle just out of the oven or warm them the day after with a dash of milk.

NOTE: If fresh porcini are hard to come by, try a combination of cremini, chanterelle, oyster, shiitake, or portobello mushrooms plus 1 ounce/28 g dried porcini to enhance the mushroom flavor. Soak the dried porcini in water for about 30 minutes, then discard the water, squeeze them, chop them, and add them to the pan along with the other mushrooms.

cascioni alle erbette

GREENS-STUFFED CASCIONI

Makes 6 cascioni

FOR THE CASCIONI

- 2 cups plus 3 tablespoons/300 g all-purpose flour, plus more for rolling
- 1 teaspoon baking powder
- Scant ⅔ cup/150 ml lukewarm water
- ¼ cup/60 ml extra-virgin olive oil
- 1 teaspoon fine sea salt

FOR THE FILLING

- 4 pounds/1.8 kg mixed greens (such as spinach, Swiss chard, broccoli rabe, or dandelion), boiled and squeezed (about 2 pounds/900 g cooked)
- ¼ cup/60 ml extra-virgin olive oil
- ½ medium yellow onion, minced (about 100 g)
- 2 garlic cloves, smashed and peeled
- Fine sea salt
- Red pepper flakes
- ½ ounce/14 g Parmigiano Reggiano cheese, finely grated (about ¼ cup firmly packed)

During one of my first vacations with friends on the Riviera Romagnola, we found ourselves in a piadineria tucked away in the hills near Gabicce. It was rustic, informal, and unassuming. We tried the cascioni—a dish much like the ubiquitous local piadina, or flatbread sandwich, but sealed; stuffed with fillings like sautéed greens, potatoes, cheese, or tomatoes; and cooked in a hot skillet until golden and charred in spots. These days, I often make cascioni at home, doubling the recipe to freeze extras for quick, satisfying lunches or snacks.

MAKE THE CASCIONI: In a large bowl, whisk together the flour and baking powder. Add the lukewarm water, olive oil, and salt, stirring with a fork until the mixture forms coarse crumbs. Transfer to a clean work surface and gather the crumbs into a cohesive ball.

Knead the dough by hand until it feels smooth, silky, and slightly springy, about 10 minutes. (If you prefer, use a stand mixer fitted with the dough hook. Knead for 5 minutes on low speed, then finish by hand for an additional 5 minutes.)

Wrap the dough in plastic wrap and let it rest at room temperature for 30 minutes.

WHILE THE CASCIONE DOUGH IS RESTING, MAKE THE FILLING: Ensure the cooked greens are thoroughly squeezed to remove any excess moisture, then roughly chop them and set aside.

Warm the olive oil in a large skillet over medium-low heat. Add the onion, garlic, and a generous pinch of salt, which helps draw out moisture and prevent burning. Stir in pepper flakes to taste, to add a subtle heat without overwhelming the other flavors.

Cook the aromatics, stirring often, until the onion becomes soft and translucent, about 8 minutes.

Add the chopped greens and toss to coat them in the flavored oil. Increase the heat to medium and cook, stirring occasionally, until the greens are dry and glistening with oil, 10 to 15 minutes. Taste and adjust the seasoning with salt as needed. Discard the garlic cloves and let the mixture cool completely before using. When cooled, mix in the grated Parmigiano.

-recipe continues-

Divide the rested dough into 6 equal pieces and roll each piece into a tight ball. Cover the dough balls with plastic wrap and let them rest for another 30 minutes at room temperature.

To assemble the cascioni, lightly flour a clean work surface and roll out one ball of dough into a paper-thin disk about 9½ inches/24 cm in diameter. Spoon one-sixth of the cooled filling onto half of the disk, spreading it evenly but leaving a ⅜-inch/1 cm border. Fold the dough over to form a crescent shape, then fold and press the edges to seal. Crimp the edges with the tines of a fork for an extra-secure seal. Repeat with the remaining dough and filling to make 6 cascioni.

Heat a 12-inch/30 cm nonstick or cast-iron skillet over medium heat. Ensure the heat is moderate; if it's too high, the cascioni may char before the dough cooks through.

Add the cascioni to the skillet two at a time, ensuring they have enough space. Cook until golden and lightly charred in spots, 10 to 15 minutes, flipping halfway through. For the final 2 minutes, stand the cascioni on their flat edges to crisp them up, using spatulas to hold them steady if needed. Transfer the cooked cascioni to a tray and cover them with a clean kitchen towel to keep warm while you cook the remaining cascioni.

Serve the cascioni warm or at room temperature. Any leftovers can be wrapped in a kitchen towel and kept for up to 2 days. Reheat gently in a hot skillet before serving.

VARIATIONS

Try filling cascioni with mashed potatoes and sausage for a hearty twist, mozzarella and crushed tomatoes for a pizza-inspired filling, or go sweet with a delightful combination of ricotta and chocolate spread.

involtini di verza

STUFFED CABBAGE ROLLS

Serves 4 as a main course

- 8 fresh Savoy cabbage leaves
- 1 ¼ pounds/570 g baking potatoes (about 2 medium), such as russet, peeled and cut into chunks
- 1 pound/450 g fresh sweet or hot Italian sausage
- 8 ounces/225 g provolone cheese, cubed
- 1 teaspoon fine sea salt
- Freshly ground black pepper
- ½ cup/120 ml extra-virgin olive oil
- 2 ounces/56 g Parmigiano Reggiano cheese, finely grated (about 1 cup firmly packed)

NOTE: Don't let the inner leaves of the Savoy cabbage go to waste. Use them to make the cozy Savoy Cabbage and Potato Soup with Mustard and Cheesy Croutons (page 55).

Cabbage rolls are a classic dish from northern Italy, particularly cherished in Lombardy and Piedmont. In Bergamo they are known as nùsecc, and in Piedmont, they are affectionately called capunet—little capons—because their plump shape resembles the rounded breast of a capon. While the traditional version features a meat-heavy filling, I prefer to use meat as a seasoning rather than the main ingredient. Instead, I turn to mashed potatoes—leftover mash works wonderfully—enriched with fresh pork sausage and provolone cheese.

Bring a large pot of water to a boil. Rinse the cabbage leaves and blanch them for about 3 minutes: You want to soften them, not cook them completely. Drain and lay flat on a clean kitchen towel.

In another pot, cover the potatoes with cold water, bring to a boil, and cook until fork-tender, 20 to 25 minutes.

Drain the potatoes, transfer them to a large bowl, and mash them with a fork or potato masher, or pass them through a ricer or a food mill.

Remove the sausage casings and crumble the meat into a nonstick skillet. Cook the sausage over medium heat, stirring occasionally, until golden brown, 5 to 7 minutes. With a spatula, transfer the sausage and the rendered fat into the mashed potatoes, then fold the ingredients together. Add the cubed provolone. Season with the salt and pepper to taste.

Preheat the oven to 400°F/200°C. Pour ¼ cup/60 ml of the olive oil into the bottom of an 8-inch/20 cm square baking dish.

To make the cabbage rolls, lay a cabbage leaf on a cutting board, keeping the midrib on the bottom side. If it is still too stiff to roll, shave the rib with a knife. Scoop one-eighth of the filling onto the middle of each leaf. Now think of the cabbage roll as if it were an envelope. First, fold up the bottom of the leaf, then fold the two sides over the filling. Roll to close. Place the little parcel seam side down in the prepared baking dish and continue with the rest.

When all the parcels are arranged cozily in the baking dish, sprinkle them with the grated Parmigiano and drizzle with the remaining ¼ cup/60 ml olive oil.

Transfer the pan to the hot oven and bake until golden, about 30 minutes. If you want to further brown the top, pop the cabbage rolls under the broiler for 5 more minutes. Serve them immediately.

Keep the leftovers in the fridge for up to 3 days. Gently reheat them in a hot oven; you want to melt the cheese again before serving.

PRE SER VED

Capturing the essence of each season by using preserving techniques such as pickling, canning, and oil-packing means you can enjoy your seasonal produce for longer. From sun-dried tomatoes to sweet onion and apple jam, these pantry staples bring bursts of flavor to your meals year-round.

carciofini sott'olio

BABY ARTICHOKES PRESERVED IN OLIVE OIL

Makes three or four ½-pint/250 ml jars

- 2 lemons
- 4 pounds/1.8 kg baby artichokes
- 6 cups/about 1.5 L white wine vinegar
- 2 tablespoons coarse sea salt
- 1 cup/240 ml extra-virgin olive oil, plus more as needed
- 15 black peppercorns
- 3 bay leaves

At the peak of spring, the Italian markets are flooded with carciofini, miniature artichokes that are picked for one single purpose: seasonal preserving. When you receive the gift of a jar of baby artichokes preserved in olive oil, know that you must be a very special friend to that person. Because it takes time, patience, and dedication to trim a whole bag of carciofini that will leave you with just a couple of jars of artichoke hearts. After trimming them, blanch them in water and vinegar, drain them, and dry them completely on a kitchen towel. The last step calls for sterilized jars and good-quality extra-virgin olive oil.

I always keep a few jars of preserved baby artichokes in my pantry for improvised aperitivo with friends. Lay out your table with enough crusty bread or focaccia for everyone and add some aged pecorino and a jar of your preserved carciofini. This spread will set the tone for a gorgeous meal with a relaxed Italian vibe.

Fill a large bowl with water and squeeze in the juice of the lemons, then add the squeezed halves to the bowl.

Remove the hardest outer leaves of an artichoke, until you reach the heart, which has lighter and tender leaves. Trim off the prickly tips of the artichoke leaves and trim the stem and base. Rub the artichoke with a lemon half and plunge the artichoke heart into the bowl of lemon water. Do the same for all the baby artichokes.

Combine the vinegar and 6 cups/about 1.5 L water in a large pot. Cover and bring to a boil over high heat. Remove the artichokes from the lemon water and add them, and the salt, to the boiling water. Reduce the heat so the liquid is simmering and cook the artichokes until they are soft enough to pierce easily with the tip of a knife, 5 to 10 minutes. It might take longer depending on how fresh your artichokes are.

Drain the pot into a colander set in the sink. Line a baking sheet with a clean kitchen towel and arrange the artichokes with tongs, standing, stems up. Cover with a second clean kitchen towel, allow them to cool to room temperature, then refrigerate overnight.

Have ready three or four sterilized ½-pint/250 ml jars. Pour a few tablespoons of olive oil into each jar, then fill them with the artichokes, packing them tightly. Add 5 peppercorns and a bay leaf to each jar. Fill the jars with olive oil, adding enough to cover the

NOTE: Choose good-quality extra-virgin olive oil to preserve the baby artichokes, as you'll be able to use that olive oil to dress a salad, drizzle over a bruschetta, or serve along with the carciofini. Not a single drop of it will be wasted.

artichokes. Let stand for a few hours, then check the jars to see if the artichokes are still covered in oil. Add more olive oil as necessary to completely cover the artichokes and tightly seal each jar.

To preserve the jars, follow the method in Preserving in a Boiling-Water Bath (see below). Let the baby artichokes cure for 1 week before using.

VARIATION:

Preserved Grilled Baby Artichokes

To impart an extra layer of flavor to carciofini, once blanched and drained, halve them and grill them on a very hot ridged cast-iron grill pan until you can see char marks. Let them cool completely, then preserve them with olive oil as in the recipe.

PRESERVING IN A BOILING-WATER BATH

TO ENSURE SAFE STORAGE, jars should be processed in a boiling-water bath. First, before filling the jars, make sure they are sterilized. Then, once they are filled, follow the steps below:

1. Fill a large pot with water and bring it to a rolling boil. Place a rack or a folded kitchen towel at the bottom of the pot to prevent the jars from touching the direct heat.
2. Carefully lower the sealed jars into the boiling water, making sure they are fully submerged, with at least 1 inch/2.5 cm of water above the tops. Cover the pot and let the jars boil for 20 minutes.
3. Use tongs to remove the jars from the pot and set them on a kitchen towel. Let them cool completely at room temperature without disturbing them.
4. After cooling, check that the lids have sealed properly—press the center of each lid; it should not pop back when pressed. If a jar hasn't sealed, store it in the refrigerator and use within 4 to 5 days.

Properly sealed jars can be stored in a cool, dark place for up to 1 year. Once you open a jar, store it in the refrigerator for 4 to 5 days, or as directed in the recipe, and make sure to top off the jar as necessary to keep the contents submerged in oil.

pomarola

TUSCAN TOMATO SAUCE

Makes three or four ½-pint/ 250 ml jars (see Notes)

- 4½ pounds/2 kg Roma (plum) tomatoes
- ½ cup/120 ml extra-virgin olive oil
- 2 medium carrots, peeled and sliced
- 2 medium celery stalks, sliced
- 1 large red onion, sliced
- 1 garlic clove, minced
- Coarse sea salt
- Handful of basil leaves

NOTES:

- The tomato sauce yield is highly dependent on the ripeness of the tomatoes and on the weather.
- Don't discard the tomato water. Use it to give flavor to soups or in place of stock in risotto, like the Roasted Tomato Orzotto (page 165). It can be stored in a bottle in the fridge for a couple of days or frozen for up to 4 months.
- If you do not have a food mill, use an immersion blender to blend the tomato sauce, then pass it through a sieve to remove any remaining seeds or skin.

Pomarola is the taste of a Tuscan summer captured in a jar. This rustic tomato sauce, born from vegetable gardens overflowing with ripe tomatoes, onions, carrots, celery, and basil, is the essence of simplicity. Every nonna has her own version, passed down through generations like a cherished family secret. My recipe mirrors the one my mum makes every summer. Her secret? A knob of butter added to the sauce at the very last minute while tossing with pasta to create a silky, creamy coating that clings lovingly to each strand.

Rinse the tomatoes, cut them in half, and remove the seeds. Transfer them to a large pot. Add the olive oil, carrots, celery, onion, garlic, and 2 tablespoons salt. Cover and simmer over low heat, stirring occasionally, until the carrots are soft and the tomatoes can easily be mashed with a wooden spoon, about 40 minutes.

Pour everything into a colander set over a bowl to collect the tomato water (see Notes).

Set a food mill over a pot and little by little puree all the vegetables; a thick, bright red sauce will fall into the pot, and you will be left with just tomato skins in the food mill (see Notes).

Return the pot to the heat and simmer for 5 minutes or longer, to thicken the sauce to your liking. Taste and adjust with salt, if needed. Then add the basil leaves, torn with your hands.

You can use the sauce immediately to dress a bowl of pasta or let it cool, then ladle it into airtight containers or glass jars and store in the fridge for up to 1 week or freeze. (Alternatively, ladle the sauce into zip-top freezer storage bags. Press out the air from the bags, seal them, and lay flat on a baking sheet. Transfer to the freezer and freeze until solid, then stack in the freezer.)

peperoncini piccanti ripieni di tonno

TUNA-STUFFED HOT CHERRY PEPPERS

Makes three 1-pint/500 ml jars

- 30 small round hot cherry peppers (about 1 pound/ 500 g total)
- 2 cups/480 ml white wine vinegar
- 1 tablespoon coarse sea salt
- Two 5-ounce/142 g jars or cans good-quality tuna
- 6 anchovy fillets
- 1 tablespoon brined or salt-packed capers, rinsed
- ½ garlic clove
- 10 fresh mint leaves
- 1¼ cups/300 ml extra-virgin olive oil, plus more as needed

NOTES: If fresh hot cherry peppers are difficult to find, jarred brined cherry peppers are the best substitute. Stem and seed them, then arrange them on a towel as described in the recipe. If the peppers are particularly large, consider doubling the tuna filling or just making a smaller batch of generously stuffed peppers.

In the depths of winter, opening a jar of these vibrant stuffed hot cherry peppers instantly brings color, warmth, and a hint of sunshine to the table. Choose good-quality extra-virgin olive oil to preserve the cherry peppers, as you'll be able to use the olive oil remaining in the jar to dress a salad, drizzle over a bruschetta, or stir-fry vegetables.

Rinse the cherry peppers, then, using disposable kitchen gloves to protect your hands, remove the stem with a paring knife and all the seeds with a teaspoon. Clean them thoroughly, as the remaining seeds will make them too hot.

Combine the vinegar, 2 cups/480 ml water, and the salt in a medium saucepan. Cover and bring to a boil over high heat. When the water is boiling, plunge the peppers into the hot water and submerge them with a wooden spoon. Cook until slightly softened but still retaining their shape, 6 to 8 minutes.

Drain the whole pot into a colander set in the sink. Line a wire rack with a clean kitchen towel and arrange the peppers with tongs, stem side down. Cover with a second clean kitchen towel, allow to cool to room temperature, and let them dry overnight.

The following day, drain the tuna and transfer to a blender or a food processor. Add the anchovy fillets, capers, garlic, and mint leaves and blend until smooth. If the filling is too thick, add a spoonful of olive oil to make it smoother and softer.

Using a small spoon, stuff the peppers to the brim with the tuna filling, then smooth the top.

Have ready three sterilized 1-pint/500 ml jars. Pack the stuffed peppers snugly into the jars and then cover them completely with oil, adding more oil as needed. Let stand for a few hours at room temperature, then check the jars, adding more oil as necessary to completely cover the peppers.

Close the jars and let the stuffed peppers cure for 1 week in the fridge before using, then store them in the refrigerator for up to 3 months.

To serve, remove the stuffed cherry peppers from the jar and place them on a plate. Let them come to room temperature before eating them. Top off the jar with more oil if necessary.

TOP: Sweet Onion & Apple Jam
BOTTOM: Tuna-Stuffed Hot Cherry Peppers

confettura di pomodori piccante

SPICY TOMATO JAM

Makes three or four ½-pint/250 ml jars

- 4½ pounds/2 kg Roma (plum) tomatoes
- 2½ cups/500 g sugar
- ½ cup/120 ml apple cider vinegar
- 1 teaspoon ground cumin
- ¼ teaspoon ground cloves
- 1 fresh Fresno chile pepper, seeded and cut into strips, or ½ teaspoon red pepper flakes

NOTES:

- For shelf-stable jam: Follow the method in Preserving in a Boiling-Water Bath (page 218).

  The jam will keep in a cool, dark place for 1 year. Once you open a jar, use what you need and keep the remaining jam in the fridge for a couple of weeks.

- For freezer jam: Let the jam cool and then ladle it into airtight containers or glass jars and freeze it.

I first made this spicy tomato jam during the whirlwind weeks leading up to our wedding. Amid the chaos of planning, I carved out a couple of hours for one of my favorite calming, mindful activities: preserving the season. The deep ruby hue and sweet heat of this jam captures the essence of late-summer tomatoes, kissed by chile and warmed by cumin and cloves, and all the anticipation for such an exciting day. We jarred the spicy tomato jam for serving at our reception, pairing it with aged local pecorino and crusty bread, alongside some Sweet Onion and Apple Jam (page 234).

Place a saucer in the freezer; you will use it to test the jam.

To peel the tomatoes, rinse them and use a sharp knife to cut an X in the skin on the blossom end.

Set up a large bowl of ice and water and keep near the stove. Bring a pot of water to a boil, and as soon as it boils, remove it from the heat and plunge the tomatoes into the water. Leave the tomatoes in the hot water for 5 minutes or until the skin starts to pull apart from the carved X. Drain the tomatoes and plunge them immediately into the ice bath.

Peel the tomatoes, halve them, remove the seeds, and transfer them to a colander. Let them drain for at least 30 minutes so that they lose most of their water.

Transfer the tomatoes to a pot and cook the pulp over medium heat for about 10 minutes, stirring occasionally to prevent the tomatoes from burning. Stir in the sugar, vinegar, cumin, cloves, and chile pepper. Continue to simmer over medium heat, stirring occasionally, until the tomatoes start to collapse, about 20 minutes.

Remove the tomatoes from the heat and puree them with an immersion blender until smooth. Return the pot to medium heat and simmer the jam until thick and glossy, 5 additional minutes. Test the jam by pouring a drop onto the frozen saucer. If after a few seconds the jam is thick and slides slowly, it is ready; otherwise, return it to the stove to cook for a few more minutes.

Have ready three or four sterilized ½-pint/250 ml jars. Pour the jam into the jars and tightly seal each jar with a lid.

giardiniera

MIXED PICKLED VEGETABLES

Makes four 1-pint/500 ml jars

- 8½ cups/2 L white wine vinegar
- ¾ cup/150 g sugar
- 3 tablespoons plus 1 teaspoon/60 g fine sea salt
- ½ head cauliflower (about 1 pound/450 g), separated into small florets
- 6 spring onions, cut into wedges, or 2 large shallots
- 2 celery stalks, thinly sliced
- 3 medium carrots, peeled and thinly sliced
- 2 bell peppers, one red and one yellow, cut into strips
- 8 ounces/225 g green beans, stem end trimmed, cut into ¾-inch/2 cm pieces
- 4 bay leaves
- 4 teaspoons black peppercorns
- 4¼ cups/1 L extra-virgin olive oil (you may not use it all)

NOTE: Choose good-quality extra-virgin olive oil to preserve the giardiniera, as you'll be able to use that olive oil to dress a salad, drizzle over a bruschetta, or stir-fry vegetables.

Giardiniera is a colorful collection of pickled vegetables—an Italian vegetable garden enclosed in a jar. You can use countless vegetables, depending on the season. I usually make mine in summer, when produce is abundant and affordable, and I always try to add some cauliflower, as I find it irresistible when pickled.

Start by choosing your favorite vegetables. You can even make a one-ingredient giardiniera, playing with colors: Cauliflower in different hues works beautifully. Clean, cut, and blanch the vegetables in vinegar and water, then drain and dry well. Arrange the vegetables in sterilized jars and cover them with extra-virgin olive oil. Now comes the hard part: The giardiniera has to cure, so you should wait at least a week before eating (a few months is even better).

Serve giardiniera as an antipasto together with a charcuterie board, along with a basket of crusty bread, use it to dress a potato salad, or make an Italian rice salad (see How to Make Insalata di Riso, page 228).

Pour the vinegar, 4¼ cups/1 L water, the sugar, and salt into a large saucepan. Stir to dissolve, cover, and bring to a boil.

When the water is boiling, blanch each vegetable separately for 3 to 5 minutes, until al dente. Scoop the vegetables with a slotted spoon and drain in a colander. Spread on a baking sheet lined with a clean kitchen towel and let completely dry at room temperature for a few hours.

To speed things up, use the residual heat of your oven if you've recently baked.

Have ready four sterilized 1-pint/500 ml jars. Arrange the vegetables in the jars, layering them so there's a little of each type of vegetable in each jar, compressing the vegetables lightly as you add them, to fill any empty space. Add a bay leaf and a teaspoon of black peppercorns to each jar.

Pour in olive oil to cover the vegetables completely. Check again after a few hours to see if you need to add more olive oil to completely cover the giardiniera.

Tightly seal each jar and follow the method in Preserving in a Boiling-Water Bath (page 218).

Let the giardiniera cure for 1 week before using, then store in the pantry, or in a dry, cool, and dark place, for up to 1 year.

-recipe continues-

Once you open a jar, store it in the refrigerator and make sure to top off the jar as necessary to keep the vegetables submerged in oil. Use within 4 to 5 days.

HOW TO MAKE INSALATA DI RISO

Serves 8 to 10

One 1-pint/500 ml jar giardiniera, store-bought or homemade (see page 226)

Fine sea salt

2¼ cups/450 g short-grain rice, such as Arborio or Carnaroli

4 ounces/115 g prosciutto cotto or cooked ham, diced (about ¾ cup)

¼ cup/30 g Taggiasca or Kalamata olives, rinsed and pitted

2 tablespoons brined or salt-packed capers, thoroughly rinsed

Extra-virgin olive oil (if not using homemade giardiniera)

2 large hard-boiled eggs

Fresh basil leaves

This short-grain rice salad, the star of many picnics and effortless summer meals, is dressed with giardiniera, a couple of hard-boiled eggs, cubed prosciutto cotto, and fresh cheese. Make it in advance and keep it in the fridge until time to eat.

Drain the jar of giardiniera, reserving the oil if using homemade.

Cook the rice in a pot of boiling salted water over medium heat until al dente. Drain and run under cold water to stop the cooking.

Transfer the rice to a large salad bowl and add the giardiniera, prosciutto cotto, olives, and capers. Use some of the reserved giardiniera oil to dress the salad, if homemade; otherwise, drizzle some extra-virgin olive oil to dress it.

Mash the hard-boiled eggs in a small bowl with a fork and add them to the rice salad along with some basil, torn with your hands. Give the rice salad a good stir, cover with plastic wrap, and stash in the fridge for a few hours before serving. Let the rice salad come back to mostly room temperature after it has been in the fridge, taste again to adjust the seasoning, and refresh with a drizzle of olive oil if it looks a bit too dry. It will keep in an airtight container in the fridge for a few days.

NOTES:

- Unlike the classic Italian rice salad of the 1980s, there is no mayonnaise here. Instead, when you mash the hard-boiled eggs into the rice, they marry with the extra-virgin olive oil to create a lighter but equally creamy dressing.
- Omit the prosciutto cotto if you want to make a vegetarian rice salad, or swap in the same amount of chopped sun-dried tomatoes (see facing page).

pomodori secchi sott'olio

SUN-DRIED TOMATOES IN OIL

Makes three ½-pint/250 ml jars

- ½ cup/ 120 ml white wine vinegar
- 1 pound/ 450 g dry-pack sun-dried tomatoes (not oil-packed), preferably San Marzano
- 1 ½ cups/ 360 ml extra-virgin olive oil (you may not use it all)
- 3 teaspoons brined or salt-packed capers, thoroughly rinsed
- 3 garlic cloves
- 3 teaspoons dried oregano

NOTE: Choose good-quality extra-virgin olive oil to preserve the sun-dried tomatoes, as you'll be able to use that olive oil to dress a salad, drizzle over a bruschetta, or stir-fry vegetables.

The weekly market in Porto Cesareo, Salento, is my personal slice of heaven. I stock up on provisions: tiny salt-packed capers bursting with flavor, dried oregano from the rocky coastline, local almonds, pitch-black baked olives, and piles of sun-dried tomatoes. These tomatoes, dried under the relentless summer sun yet still chewy, are piled high on the stalls among taralli and nuts.

Once home, I rehydrate the tomatoes in a pot of boiling acidulated water, a simple ritual that revives their texture. Then I pack them snugly into jars and cover with extra-virgin olive oil infused with all the scents of the Mediterranean: garlic, oregano, and capers. I leave them in the jars for months, giving the tomatoes time to absorb all the flavors. I toss them into salads, cook them with vegetables for an extra hit of flavor, or serve them as part of an appetizer spread.

Pour 8 cups/1.9 L water and the vinegar into a large saucepan, cover, and bring to a boil over high heat.

When the water is boiling, plunge the tomatoes and cook until you're able to easily tear off a piece of tomato and they no longer have a rubbery texture, 3 to 5 minutes, depending on how dry they were initially.

Drain the whole pot into a colander set in the sink. Spread the tomatoes on a baking sheet lined with a clean kitchen towel. Let stand for a few hours at room temperature until they are completely dry. If you want to speed up the process, you can use the residual heat of your oven, if you have baked something in the meantime.

Have ready 3 sterilized ½-pint/250 ml jars. Pour a few tablespoons of olive oil into each jar, then fill them with the tomatoes, packing them tightly. Add a teaspoon of capers, a clove of garlic, and a teaspoon of dried oregano to each jar. Fill the jars with olive oil, adding enough to cover the tomatoes. Let stand for a few hours, then check the jars, adding more olive oil as necessary to completely cover the tomatoes.

Tightly seal each jar and follow the method in Preserving in a Boiling-Water Bath (page 218).

Let the tomatoes cure for 1 week before using, then store them in the pantry, or a dry, cool, and dark place, for up to 1 year.

Once you open a jar, store it in the refrigerator and top it off as necessary to keep the tomatoes submerged in oil. Use within 4 to 5 days.

Millefiori

confettura di zucca

SQUASH JAM

Makes four or five 4- to 5-ounce/ 120 to 150 ml jars

2¼ pounds/ 1 kg acorn squash, butternut squash, Mantovana squash, or pumpkin, peeled, seeded, and cut into chunks

Juice of 1 clementine

1 tablespoon fresh lemon juice

1½ cups/ 300 g sugar

1 cinnamon stick

1 vanilla bean, split lengthwise

NOTE: If you don't have a steaming basket, here's how to steam the squash. Use a fine-mesh sieve with a long handle set over a pot or Dutch oven, keeping it covered while steaming. Alternatively, use the microwave: Place the squash in a microwave-safe bowl with 2 tablespoons of water. Cover with plastic wrap or a lid and microwave for 3 minutes. If not fork-tender, continue cooking in 30-second increments until done.

This unusual squash jam makes the most of the seasonal abundance. It has the same mellow sweetness of a chestnut puree but with the bright citrusy notes of clementine and lemon juice. It's perfect for spreading on buttered toast, pairing with aged, sharp cheese, or even using as a topping for your morning yogurt.

Place the squash chunks in a steaming basket set over a pot (see Note). Pour 1 cup/240 ml water into the pot and steam the squash over medium heat until the squash flesh is soft enough to pierce easily with a knife, 25 to 30 minutes.

Transfer the cooked squash pulp to a medium pot and mash it roughly with a potato masher. Add the clementine juice, lemon juice, sugar, and cinnamon stick. Scrape in the vanilla seeds and add the pod, too. Stir everything together until the sugar begins to dissolve.

Place the pot over medium heat and cook, stirring frequently with a wooden spoon to further mash the squash and create a smooth puree. Unlike most jams, this one starts out quite thick, so keep an eye on it. Continue cooking until thick, jammy, smooth, and fragrant, about 10 minutes.

Discard the cinnamon stick and vanilla pod.

Let the jam cool and then ladle it into airtight containers or glass jars and store it in the fridge for up to a couple of weeks or freeze it.

confettura di cipolle di tropea e mele

SWEET ONION & APPLE JAM

Makes six or seven 4- to 5-ounce/120 to 150 ml jars

- 2¼ pounds/1 kg sweet Tropea onions or Vidalia onions
- 2 large Gala apples (about 8 ounces/225 g each)
- 10 black peppercorns
- 2 whole cloves
- 4 juniper berries (see Note)
- 2 tablespoons extra-virgin olive oil
- ¼ teaspoon red pepper flakes
- ¼ teaspoon ground cinnamon
- 1 bay leaf
- Fine sea salt
- ⅓ cup/80 ml red wine vinegar
- 2 cups/400 g sugar

Sweet and savory, sharp and mellow, earthy and bright—this jam is a play on contrasts, balancing the caramelized depth of slow-cooked onions with the natural sweetness and acidity of apples. The result is something far greater than the sum of its parts: a jam that brings out the best in cheese, cutting through the richness of aged pecorino or enhancing the nuttiness of Parmigiano.

Apples and onions have always belonged together. Both are storage crops, or ingredients meant to last through winter, tucked away in pantries and cellars. Together, they create a jam that's equally at home on a cheese board, layered into a sandwich, and paired with roasted meats.

Place a saucer in the freezer; you will use it to test the jam.

Peel the onions and slice them very thinly. Use a mandoline slicer rather than a knife, if you have one, which will save time and tears. Place all the onions in a large heavy-bottomed pot. Peel and grate the apples and add them to the onions.

Using a mortar and pestle, crush the peppercorns, cloves, and juniper berries into a fine powder. Add them to the sliced onions and apples along with the olive oil, pepper flakes, cinnamon, bay leaf, and a generous pinch of salt.

Sweat the onions over low heat, stirring them from time to time, until soft and translucent, about 30 minutes. Pour in the vinegar and cook the onions until the vinegar has completely evaporated, 5 to 8 minutes.

Add the sugar, stirring thoroughly to dissolve it. Keep cooking the jam until the onions have reduced by half and when you drag a spoon across the bottom of the pot there is no more liquid, 45 to 50 minutes.

Remove the bay leaf and juniper berries, then roughly puree the jam with an immersion blender. Return the jam to the stove and simmer until thick and glossy, about 5 more minutes. Test the jam by pouring a drop onto the frozen saucer. If after a few seconds the jam is thick and slides slowly, it is ready; otherwise, set it back on the stove for a few more minutes.

Have ready six or seven sterilized 4- to 5-ounce/120 to 150 ml jars. Pour the jam into the jars and tightly seal each jar with a lid.

NOTE: Juniper berries have a woody, evergreen flavor. They remind me of the surrounding woods, where they grow in large, prickly, aromatic shrubs. While they are often paired with game, I love incorporating them into my spice mix for their unique depth. If juniper berries are difficult to find, try using two rosemary sprigs stripped of their needles—the woody stalk will lend a similarly pleasant, earthy aroma. Remove the juniper along with the bay leaf before pureeing the jam.

FOR SHELF-STABLE JAM: Follow the method in Preserving in a Boiling-Water Bath (page 218).

The jam will keep in a cool, dark place for 1 year. Once you open a jar, use what you need and keep the remaining jam in the fridge for a couple of weeks.

FOR FREEZER JAM: Let the jam cool and then ladle it into airtight containers or glass jars and freeze it.

ODE TO THE FOOD MILL

A FOOD MILL IS A TIMELESS HAND-CRANKED TOOL whose sturdy simplicity makes it ideal for everyday cooking. It features a stainless steel funnel-shaped bowl and a hand-crank mechanism, and typically includes a set of three milling discs, allowing you to control how fine or coarse the food is milled. Equipped with three foldable legs, it securely rests over bowls and pots. Designed for mashing, pureeing, and straining, it transforms boiled potatoes into pillowy gnocchi (see page 114) or into a light, fluffy puree without risking a gluey mess.

My grandma would set a pot on the table and securely place the food mill on top. Hunched over her setup, she'd begin turning the mill's handle with an almost hypnotic rhythm, moving clockwise for a long time until a single counterclockwise turn became necessary to dislodge the skins stuck at the bottom. She would pull the pot closer to her, almost holding it steady with her body, as if she were embracing the food she was preparing. The wisdom of those repeated gestures, the rhythm and sound of the food mill, are part of an unwritten code of Italian cooking—a code etched in my memory, made up of vivid images and shared moments.

The food mill is one of the most essential tools for making la salsa—the traditional tomato puree typically prepared in large quantities by entire households. A good food mill is also the go-to for preparing a small batch of pomarola (see page 221), the ruby-red Tuscan tomato sauce flavored with carrots, celery, onion, and fresh herbs. The same goes for jams and preserves. You can make the silkiest pitch-black blackberry jam with a food mill, turning it tirelessly to squeeze out every last bit of fruit and leave the seeds behind.

The food mill is just as handy for beans and chickpeas: Run them through and you'll get the smoothest, creamiest passato, a creamy soup. I like to reheat it with olive oil, garlic, and fresh herbs for an easy, comforting weeknight meal. The mill works wonders for fish soups, too, or even for making baby food, by turning vegetables into a creamy mash without adding unwanted air. I always use mine for minestrone, the classic Italian vegetable soup: Start by cooking a jumble of diced vegetables, then pass them through the mill for a velvety soup that my daughter loves to sip straight from a cup. Toss in some cooked rice or pasta, and dinner is done.

When I first moved into my own apartment, one of the very first kitchen tools I bought was a humble, reliable food mill. Now it hangs on my kitchen wall alongside a trusty colander, a beat-up secondhand aluminum pan for roasting potatoes, a grater, and a couple of wooden spoons. Every time I see these tools, I'm reminded of the basics of cooking: simple, honest meals made with just a handful of essential tools.

SW
EET
ENED

Vegetables step into the world of desserts with these playful recipes. Naturally sweet squashes and carrots, but also radicchio, cucumber, and chard, are transformed into cakes, tarts, sorbets, and confections that surprise and delight.

scarpaccia di zucchine

SWEET ZUCCHINI CAKE

Serves 8 to 12

- Softened butter, for the baking pan
- 5 tablespoons/60 g turbinado sugar
- ½ cup/120 ml whole milk
- 4 tablespoons/60 g unsalted butter
- 9 ounces/255 g zucchini (about 1 medium)
- 1 large egg
- ¾ cup plus 1 tablespoon/100 g all-purpose flour
- ⅓ cup plus 1 tablespoon/80 g granulated sugar
- ½ teaspoon baking powder
- Grated zest of ½ lemon, preferably organic
- 1 teaspoon vanilla extract
- ¼ teaspoon fine sea salt
- 8 fresh basil leaves, finely chopped
- Powdered sugar, for serving

NOTE: This recipe works especially well with slender young zucchini, about the thickness of a finger, because they have a sweeter, more delicate taste.

In Viareggio, a Tuscan coastal town, locals have long embraced the idea of desserts made with vegetables. Scarpaccia is a thin, moist cake made with zucchini and a touch of basil. The name *scarpaccia*, which means "large, ugly shoe," is a nod to its flat, rustic appearance, about as thick as an old shoe sole.

This is a humble cake, born from garden abundance. Lightly sweet, with an unusual green flavor, it remains delightfully moist thanks to finely sliced zucchini folded into a simple batter of flour, milk, egg, sugar, and butter. I like to add lemon zest and vanilla extract along with the basil to make it even more irresistible.

Position racks in the lower third and center of the oven and preheat the oven to 400°F/200°C. Line the bottom of an 8- to 9-inch/20 to 23 cm round baking pan with parchment paper. Generously butter the parchment paper and the sides of the pan and sprinkle with 3 tablespoons of the turbinado sugar. This will ensure the cake has golden, caramelized edges.

Warm the milk and unsalted butter in a small saucepan over medium heat until the butter has melted. Set aside and let cool to room temperature.

Slice the zucchini crosswise into very thin slices about 1/16 inch/2 mm thick. Transfer to a bowl and set aside.

In a large bowl, stir together the egg and the cooled-down milk mixture. Add the flour, granulated sugar, baking powder, lemon zest, vanilla, and salt. Stir well until you get a smooth and creamy batter with no lumps. Add the zucchini and basil.

Pour the batter into the prepared pan, level it with a spatula, and sprinkle with the remaining 2 tablespoons turbinado sugar.

Transfer the cake to the lower rack of the oven and bake for 15 minutes. Move to the middle rack, reduce the oven temperature to 350°F/175°C, and bake until golden brown, firm, and slightly springy to the touch, 40 to 50 minutes.

Let the cake cool in the pan on a wire rack for about 20 minutes. Invert the cake onto a plate, peel off the parchment paper, then invert the cake again onto a serving plate to cool completely.

When the scarpaccia is cool, sprinkle it with powdered sugar and serve. It keeps for a couple of days at room temperature on the counter.

torta di zucca e ricotta

RICOTTA & SQUASH CAKE

Serves 8 to 12

½ small squash (about 1 pound/450 g), such as Mantovana, kabocha, delicata, or butternut squash, seeded (see Notes)

15 to 16 ounces/425 to 450 g fresh whole-milk cow or sheep ricotta (about 2 cups)

Softened butter and rice flour (see Notes), for the baking pan

¾ cup/150 g sugar

2 tablespoons potato starch (see Notes)

Seeds scraped from 1 vanilla bean

4 large eggs

¼ cup/80 g dark chocolate and hazelnut spread

Flaky sea salt, for sprinkling

This cake, inspired by a ricotta cake that my friend Emanuela Regi bakes weekly for the Caciosteria restaurant in Pavana, is reminiscent of Italian baked cheesecake. I like to stir some roasted squash into the ricotta batter, turning it into a moist, orange-hued, vanilla-spiked cake.

Finish it with a generous smear of chocolate spread. My favorite dark chocolate spread is an Italian organic brand, Rigoni di Asiago. The gluten-free, dairy-free hazelnut and chocolate spread has a deep, intense flavor that's not too sweet, making it the perfect complement to the squash and ricotta in this cake. Don't skip the final sprinkle of flaky sea salt; it adds an irresistible contrast.

Preheat the oven to 400°F/200°C. Line a baking sheet with parchment paper.

Place the squash cut side down on the lined baking sheet. Transfer the squash to the oven and roast until you can effortlessly pierce through the skin with the tip of a knife, about 35 minutes. Remove the squash from the oven, flip it cut side up, and set aside. Once it's cool to the touch, scoop out the flesh with a spoon into a bowl, then discard the skin. You should end up with about 1⅓ cups/300 g cooked squash pulp. Let it cool completely. (The squash pulp can be prepared in advance. Keep it in an airtight container in the fridge for up to 5 days.)

Place the ricotta in a fine-mesh sieve set over a bowl. Cover with plastic wrap and let it drain in the refrigerator for about 1 hour, until firm and dry. This step ensures a creamy, dense texture in the cake.

Preheat the oven to 350°F/175°C. Generously butter an 8-inch/20 cm springform pan with a removable bottom, then dust it with rice flour, shaking out the excess. Place the prepared pan on a baking sheet to catch any potential leaks during baking.

Using a spatula, press the drained ricotta through a fine-mesh sieve into a large bowl, creating a silky base. Add the squash pulp, sugar, potato starch, and vanilla seeds. Stir with a wooden spoon until smooth.

Crack the eggs into the batter, one at a time, stirring well after each addition to ensure it's fully incorporated before adding the next. Pour the batter into the prepared pan, smoothing the surface with a spatula.

-recipe continues-

Transfer the pan to the hot oven and bake until the cake puffs up, the edges turn golden brown and gently pull away from the sides, the center glows bright orange, and it feels springy to the touch, 1 hour to 1 hour 20 minutes.

Let the cake cool in the pan completely on a wire rack before removing the sides of the springform pan. Don't worry if the center sinks slightly as it cools—this creates the perfect space for spreading chocolate hazelnut cream (or a dollop of jam, or even a drizzle of salted caramel). Transfer the cake to a serving plate.

Spread the top of the cooled cake with the dark chocolate and hazelnut spread. If the spread is too thick, gently warm it in a double boiler or place it in a bowl in a saucepan of hot water until it reaches a pourable texture. Finish with a sprinkle of flaky sea salt, which will add a subtle crunch and a hint of contrast to the sweetness.

Slice and serve at room temperature.

Wrap any leftovers tightly in aluminum foil and store them in the fridge for 3 to 4 days. Bring the cake to room temperature before serving to enjoy its full flavor and texture.

NOTES:

- This recipe works beautifully with any small-to-medium squash: delicata, acorn, butternut, kabocha, or red kuri, known for its distinct chestnut-like flavor. Roasting time will vary depending on the size and texture of the squash, so start checking after about 30 minutes. It's ready when you can easily scoop out the tender, roasted flesh with a spoon.
- This recipe uses potato starch, but you could also use all-purpose flour or cornstarch (if you need a gluten-free option). The same applies to the rice flour used to coat the pan—feel free to swap it out for all-purpose flour as needed.

bomboloni alla crema

PASTRY CREAM–FILLED DONUTS

Makes 15 to 20 bomboloni

FOR THE BOMBOLONI DOUGH

- 1 small starchy potato (about 5 ounces/ 150 g), such as a russet
- 2½ cups/ 330 g bread flour, plus more for dusting
- ⅓ cup plus 1 tablespoon/ 80 g sugar
- 2 teaspoons active dry or instant yeast
- Grated zest of 1 lemon, preferably organic
- ½ cup/ 120 ml lukewarm water
- 2 large egg yolks
- 3½ tablespoons/ 50 g unsalted butter, at room temperature
- ¼ teaspoon fine sea salt
- Extra-virgin olive oil, for greasing

FOR THE PASTRY CREAM

- 2 cups/ 480 ml whole milk
- 1 vanilla bean or 1 teaspoon vanilla extract
- ½ cup/ 100 g plus 2 tablespoons sugar
- 3 large egg yolks
- ½ cup/ 65 g cornstarch

FOR SHAPING AND FRYING

- All-purpose flour, for dusting
- ½ cup/ 100 g sugar, for coating the bomboloni
- 4¼ cups/ 1 L high-heat oil, such as sunflower oil

With their soft, fluffy dough enriched by the addition of boiled and mashed potatoes, Tuscan bomboloni are the ultimate indulgence—especially when filled with silky vanilla pastry cream and enjoyed while still warm. The best part? The satisfying crunch of sugar on your lips after the very first bite.

MAKE THE BOMBOLONI DOUGH: Scrub the potato and place it in a small pot. Fill the pot with cold water, bring it to a boil over high heat, then reduce to a simmer and cook the potato until you can easily pierce it with the tip of a knife, about 25 minutes. Drain it and run it under cold water to cool it slightly.

Peel the potato, transfer it to a plate, and mash it immediately with a fork. It's easier to do this when the potato is still steaming hot so that you'll get a smooth, fluffy mash and avoid lumps in the dough. Set the mashed potato aside to cool to lukewarm. Don't be tempted to use the potato when it is still hot, as the heat will kill the yeast, resulting in a heavy dough for your bomboloni.

In a stand mixer fitted with the dough hook, combine the flour, mashed potato, sugar, yeast, and lemon zest. Pour in the lukewarm water and begin kneading on low speed with the mixer. Gradually incorporate the egg yolks and softened butter, adding the salt last. The dough will be sticky at first, but with patience and continued kneading—about 10 minutes with the mixer—it will come together.

Lightly dust a wooden board with flour. Scrape the dough onto the board and gently knead it until it becomes smooth and elastic. Shape the dough into a ball, place it in a bowl lightly greased with olive oil, and cover with a damp cloth. Let the dough rise in a warm spot, such as an oven with the light on, until doubled in size, about 2 hours.

WHILE THE BOMBOLONI ARE PROOFING, MAKE THE PASTRY CREAM: Prepare an ice bath in a large roasting pan or your kitchen sink. Fill it halfway with cold water and plenty of ice—you'll use this later to chill the cream quickly once it's cooked.

Pour the milk into a medium saucepan. Scrape in the seeds from the vanilla bean and add the pod (or add the vanilla extract) and 2 tablespoons of the sugar. This step helps prevent the milk from

NOTE: Vanilla beans are precious, and I make the most of each of them. After steeping the pod in the pastry cream, rinse it under running water and dry it on paper towels. Once dried, stash it in a jar of sugar—it will infuse the sugar with its aroma for months. Over time, as you collect more used pods, blend them with some of the sugar to create a richly aromatic vanilla sugar, perfect for cakes and other baked goods.

scorching. Warm the milk over medium heat and remove it from the heat as soon as it begins to steam.

In another medium saucepan, whisk the egg yolks with the remaining ½ cup/100 g sugar and the cornstarch until smooth; it might take some elbow grease. Slowly pour the hot milk into the egg mixture in a thin stream, whisking constantly to prevent curdling.

Place the egg-milk mixture over medium-low heat and cook, whisking constantly. As soon as large, slow bubbles appear and the pastry cream thickens, remove it from the heat.

Transfer the pastry cream to a large, shallow bowl, cover with plastic wrap pressed directly onto the surface, and set the bowl in the ice bath. Once cooled, refrigerate until needed. (The pastry cream can be prepared a day in advance.)

SHAPE AND FRY THE BOMBOLONI: When the dough has doubled, lightly flour a wooden board. Transfer the dough onto the board, flatten it gently, and use a rolling pin to roll it to about a ⅜-inch/1 cm thickness.

Use a 3-inch/8 cm round cookie cutter to cut out the bomboloni, setting them aside on a generously floured surface. Gather the scraps, knead briefly, and roll out again to cut more rounds.

Lightly dust the bomboloni with flour, cover with a cloth, and let them rise until plump and doubled in thickness, 1 to 2 hours.

Pour the sugar onto a shallow plate. Set a wire rack on a baking sheet and keep near the stove. Pour 3 inches/about 7 cm oil into a large, deep pan and warm over medium-high heat to 320°F/160°C on a deep-frying thermometer. The oil should be deep enough for the bomboloni to float, ensuring the characteristic pale ring around the center.

Working in batches to avoid overcrowding, fry the bomboloni until golden brown on the first side, about 3 minutes. Flip them gently to brown the other side, another 3 minutes. Lift them out with a slotted spoon and place them on the wire rack to drain.

While still hot, transfer the bomboloni to the plate of sugar, turning them to coat evenly on all sides.

Remove the pastry cream from the fridge, take out the vanilla pod (don't discard it; see Note), and whisk the cream until smooth and silky. Don't skip this step or you'll end up with a lumpy cream. Transfer the cream to a piping bag fitted with a round tip. Insert the tip into the side of each bombolone and fill generously with the pastry cream.

Serve immediately. Bomboloni are best enjoyed fresh—messy and delicious!

torta variegata alla zucca e cacao

MARBLED SQUASH & COCOA CAKE

Serves 8 to 12

Softened butter and flour, for the loaf pan

3 large eggs

¾ cup plus 2 tablespoons/ 175 g sugar

1 ⅓ cups/ 300 g roasted squash (see page 242)

½ cup/ 125 g whole-milk yogurt

¼ cup plus 3 tablespoons/ 100 ml extra-virgin olive oil

1 ⅔ cups/ 208 g all-purpose flour

⅓ cup/ 50 g potato starch

1 tablespoon plus 2 teaspoons/ 16 g baking powder

½ teaspoon ground cinnamon

½ teaspoon freshly grated nutmeg

¼ teaspoon fine sea salt

Grated zest of 1 orange, preferably organic

¼ cup/ 25 g unsweetened cocoa powder

¼ cup/ 60 ml hot espresso or hot strong black coffee

NOTE: Using Dutch-process cocoa powder will give a deeper color and flavor.

When I'm not transforming roasted squash into an Italian cheesecake (see page 242), I fold squash pulp into a simple loaf cake, marbled with cocoa powder. You might also see this cake called plum cake: What is known as a loaf cake in English is referred to as plum cake in Italian, despite having absolutely nothing to do with plums!

No matter what you call it, the cake is perfect nibbled for breakfast with an espresso, or as an accompaniment to a cup of steaming tea for merenda, Italy's sacred afternoon snack.

Preheat the oven to 400°F/200°C. Butter and flour an 8½-by-4½-inch/ 22 by 12 cm loaf pan, shaking out the excess.

In a large bowl, beat the eggs and sugar with a hand or stand mixer until pale and creamy, about 5 minutes.

Stir in the roasted squash, yogurt, and olive oil until smooth.

In another bowl, sift together the flour, potato starch, baking powder, cinnamon, nutmeg, and salt. Add to the wet mixture in two increments, stirring just until combined. Fold in the orange zest.

Dissolve the cocoa powder in the hot espresso. Transfer 2 scant cups/ about 450 g of the batter into another bowl. Stir the cocoa-espresso mixture into the reserved batter until smooth and well mixed.

Pour half of the orange batter into the prepared pan. Spoon half of the cocoa batter into the center. Repeat with the remaining batters, always pouring the batter into the center of the previous layer.

To create the marbled effect, swirl gently with a skewer or knife in figure-eight motions.

Bake for 15 minutes, until a skin forms. Remove from the oven and score a long slash across the top to help the cake bloom.

Reduce the oven temperature to 350°F/175°C and bake until golden brown and a skewer inserted into the center comes out clean, 45 to 50 minutes more.

Let the cake cool in the pan on a wire rack for 20 minutes. Invert onto a plate, then flip onto a serving plate.

Store wrapped at room temperature for 3 to 4 days. Slices freeze well: Wrap in aluminum foil, place in a zip-top bag, and freeze for up to 3 months. Thaw at room temperature before serving.

FLETT
New
Seasons
APPLE & GOOSEBERRY

torta d'erbi

SWISS CHARD TART

Serves 8

FOR THE PIE DOUGH

2 cups/250 g all-purpose flour

⅔ cup/133 g sugar

¼ teaspoon fine sea salt

Grated zest of 1 orange, preferably organic

9 tablespoons/125 g unsalted butter, softened but still cold, cubed

1 large egg, beaten

FOR THE FILLING

9 ounces/250 g Swiss chard, hard stem ends removed

⅓ cup/50 g raisins

¼ cup/60 ml warm water

2 tablespoons Vin Santo or Maraschino

3½ ounces/100 g day-old bread, crusts removed

1 cup/250 ml whole milk, warm

½ cup/100 g sugar

⅓ cup/50 g pine nuts

⅓ cup/50 g candied orange peel, diced

½ teaspoon ground cinnamon

¼ teaspoon freshly grated nutmeg

2 large eggs, lightly beaten

FOR ASSEMBLY

Softened butter, for the tart pan

All-purpose flour, for rolling

The sweet dessert torta d'erbi, made with Swiss chard, hails from Lucca, Tuscany. It might sound off-putting, but once you get past the green filling, which may immediately remind you of a savory preparation, you'll be surprised by this delicately sweet, spiced cake. The predominant flavors are pine nuts, raisins, and candied orange peel—typical of Italian desserts—with a waft of cinnamon and nutmeg. Make this as a lovely, wintery treat.

MAKE THE PIE DOUGH: In a large bowl, combine the flour, sugar, salt, and orange zest. Add the cubed butter and rub it into the dry ingredients with your fingertips until the mixture resembles fine crumbs, like grated Parmigiano. (Alternatively, use a stand mixer fitted with the paddle attachment for this step.)

Add the beaten egg and use your hands to quickly incorporate all the ingredients until the dough comes together. It will still be slightly sticky, but the flour should be incorporated with no visible streaks. Flatten the dough into a disk, wrap it in plastic wrap, and stash it in the fridge to rest for a few hours, or better, until the next day. It can even be made a couple of days in advance and kept in the fridge until you're ready to make the tart.

MAKE THE FILLING: Bring a large pot of water to a boil. Add the Swiss chard and push it down with a wooden spoon to submerge it completely. Boil until tender, about 8 minutes. Drain the chard and let it cool in a colander.

While the chard cools, place the raisins in a small bowl and cover them with the warm water and Vin Santo. Let them steep for 10 minutes. In another bowl, soak the bread in the warm milk for 10 minutes, allowing it to absorb the liquid fully.

Once the chard is cool enough to handle, squeeze out as much water as possible, then finely chop it and transfer it to a large bowl. Drain and squeeze the raisins and bread, removing excess liquid, and add them to the bowl along with the sugar, half of the pine nuts, the candied orange peel, and spices. Add the beaten eggs and mix thoroughly to create a soft green batter flecked with raisins and candied peel.

-recipe continues-

ASSEMBLE THE TART: Remove the pie dough from the fridge and let it sit at room temperature for about 20 minutes to soften slightly.

Position racks in the lower third and center of the oven and preheat the oven to 350°F/175°C. Generously butter an 8- to 9-inch/20 to 23 cm tart pan with a removable bottom.

Divide the dough into two unequal portions: two-thirds of the dough and one-third. On a floured surface, roll out the larger piece of the dough into a round about 10 inches/25 cm in diameter and ¼ inch/6 mm thick. Carefully lift the dough using the rolling pin and lay it into the prepared tart pan. Press the dough gently into the bottom and about 1 inch/2.5 cm up the sides. Trim any excess dough with a sharp knife and save the scraps for later.

Prick the bottom and sides of the crust with a fork. Scrape the filling into the tart shell, spread it into an even layer, and scatter with the remaining pine nuts.

Knead the dough scraps together with the remaining smaller piece of the dough. Roll it out to a ¼-inch/6 mm thickness. Using a sharp knife, pizza cutter, or pastry wheel for decorative edges, cut the dough into strips about ⅜ inch/1 cm wide. For a more rustic look, you can vary the widths slightly, or keep them uniform for a classic finish.

Start by laying half of the strips horizontally across the tart, spacing them evenly. Gently press the ends of the strips into the edges of the tart shell to secure them. Next, create the lattice pattern by laying the remaining strips vertically across the tart. Once all the strips are placed, gently press the ends of the vertical strips into the tart edges. Trim any overhanging dough with a sharp knife to keep the edges neat and even.

Place the tart on a baking sheet and transfer to the lower rack of the oven. Bake for 30 minutes. Move the pan to the middle rack and bake until the crust is golden brown and the filling is set, an additional 15 to 20 minutes.

Let the tart cool completely on a wire rack before removing it from the pan. Slice and serve at room temperature.

The tart keeps well on the counter for 3 to 4 days.

torta di carote alpina

ALPINE CARROT CAKE

Serves 8 to 12

4 large eggs

¾ cup/ 150 g granulated sugar

9 ounces/250 g carrots, finely grated

⅓ cup/ 80 ml cold-pressed sunflower seed oil

1 cup/ 100 g almond flour

¾ cup plus 1 tablespoon/ 100 g all-purpose flour

1 tablespoon plus 1 teaspoon/ 16 g baking powder

½ teaspoon ground cinnamon

¼ teaspoon fine sea salt

FOR THE ICING

1⅓ cups/ 150 g powdered sugar

3 tablespoons fresh lemon juice

2 tablespoons sliced almonds, toasted

This carrot cake has its roots in the Italian Alps, where it was brought across the Swiss border. Light, moist, and simple to make, it boasts a short ingredients list and a delicate hint of cinnamon. When I want to make it a bit fancier, I drizzle a thin, citrusy icing over the cake. As it dries, the icing transforms into a glossy, glasslike layer that keeps the cake moist for days.

Preheat the oven to 350°F/175°C. Line an 8- to 9-inch/20 to 23 cm round baking pan with parchment paper.

In a large bowl, beat the eggs with the granulated sugar until frothy, pale, and doubled in volume. Add the finely grated carrots and sunflower seed oil and mix thoroughly. Add the almond flour, all-purpose flour, baking powder, cinnamon, and salt and fold the dry ingredients into the beaten eggs.

Pour the batter into the lined pan and transfer to the hot oven. Bake the carrot cake for 35 to 40 minutes, until golden, firm, and lightly springy to the touch.

Let the cake cool in the pan on a wire rack for about 20 minutes. Invert the cake onto a plate, peel off the parchment paper, then invert it again onto a wire rack set on a baking sheet, so the cake has a nice golden-brown baked surface on top.

PREPARE THE ICING: In a bowl, whisk the powdered sugar with lemon juice until you have a smooth, runny icing. Pour it over the cake, tilting it to evenly distribute the icing: The icing will drip off and collect on the baking sheet. Decorate the surface with the toasted sliced almonds.

Let the icing dry for a couple of hours. When completely dry, use two spatulas to lift the cake onto a serving plate.

The cake is even better after a day's rest, as the crumb tightens, the carrots soften, and the texture of the cake is even more moist. You can keep the cake on the counter for 3 to 4 days.

LEFT: Alpine Carrot Cake
RIGHT: Radicchio & White Chocolate Cake

torta ciosota al radicchio

RADICCHIO & WHITE CHOCOLATE CAKE FROM CHIOGGIA

Serves 8 to 12

- Softened butter, for the cake pan
- 1 cup/200 g granulated sugar
- 11 tablespoons/150 g unsalted butter, at room temperature, diced
- 4 large eggs, at room temperature
- 1¼ cups/160 g all-purpose flour, plus more as needed
- 1¾ cups/220 g hazelnuts, toasted (see Note)
- ⅓ cup/30 g Homemade Breadcrumbs (page 84) or panko
- 1 tablespoon plus 2 teaspoons/16 g baking powder
- 1 teaspoon vanilla extract
- ½ teaspoon freshly grated nutmeg
- ¼ teaspoon fine sea salt
- 9 ounces/250 g radicchio di Chioggia, cored and finely minced
- 5 ounces/150 g carrots, finely grated
- 3½ ounces/100 g white chocolate, chopped
- Powdered sugar (optional), for serving

The Veneto region has an incredible array of radicchio varieties, from the delicate radicchio variegato di Castelfranco, an edible rose with creamy yellow leaves with red and purple speckles, to radicchio rosso di Treviso Tardivo, the most famous and prized variety, known for its elongated shape and elegantly curled leaves with bright white ribs (see page 156).

Radicchio di Chioggia, resembling a small red cabbage with round, compact heads and white veins, is one of the most widely grown varieties in Italy. Among its many uses, it even lends its name and subtle bitterness to torta ciosota, a unique cake from Chioggia that pairs the slightly bitter radicchio with finely grated carrots, deeply toasted hazelnuts, and warming spices such as vanilla and nutmeg. To make it even more delicious, add handfuls of chopped white chocolate.

Preheat the oven to 350°F/175°C. Butter an 8- to 9-inch/20 to 23 cm round cake pan and line it with parchment paper.

In a stand mixer fitted with the paddle attachment (or in a large bowl using a hand mixer), cream the granulated sugar and diced butter until pale yellow, light, and fluffy, about 3 minutes. Scrape down the sides of the bowl with a rubber spatula as needed to ensure even mixing.

Slowly add the eggs one at a time, making sure each one is completely incorporated with the creamed butter and sugar before adding the next. If the mixture begins to curdle, add a spoonful of flour to help bring it back together.

Blend the toasted hazelnuts and breadcrumbs in a small blender until you have a fine powder. Fold them into the batter along with the flour, baking powder, vanilla, nutmeg, and salt.

Stir in the radicchio, carrots, and white chocolate until well incorporated. The batter will be dense and slightly coarse. Scrape the batter into the prepared pan and level it with a spatula.

Transfer the pan to the hot oven and bake for 50 to 55 minutes, until a toothpick inserted in the center comes out clean and the cake is golden brown, firm, and lightly springy to the touch.

Let the cake cool in the pan on a wire rack for about 20 minutes. Run a butter knife around the cake, then invert it onto a plate, peel off the parchment paper, and flip it right side up onto a serving plate. If desired, dust the cake with powdered sugar just before serving.

The cake can be stored at room temperature for a couple of days.

NOTE: Thoroughly toasting hazelnuts makes a big difference here. Even if you're using pretoasted nuts, it's worth toasting them again for a deeper, fuller aroma. Preheat the oven to 325°F/ 160°C and spread the hazelnuts on a small baking sheet. Toast them for about 20 minutes, until they turn golden brown and fill your kitchen with a rich, nutty aroma. After toasting, place the hazelnuts in a clean kitchen towel and rub off the skins. Let them cool completely before blending them with the breadcrumbs.

ITALIAN GIN

sorbetto al cetriolo corretto al gin

CUCUMBER SORBET WITH GIN

Serves 4 to 6

- 13 ounces/365 g peeled and seeded cucumber (from about 1 large cucumber)
- 3 tablespoons fresh lime juice
- ¾ cup/150 g sugar
- 4 fresh basil leaves
- 1 fresh mint leaf
- ⅔ teaspoon/2 g xantham gum (optional)
- Gin (optional), for serving

One summer, my husband, Tommaso, and I couldn't stop experimenting with our new ice cream maker. Every hot day called for a different flavor—strawberry, white peach, apricot, plum—until the garden gave us an abundance of cucumbers. This sorbet was Tommaso's idea, inspired by a dessert we once enjoyed at a local restaurant, Futura Osteria in Abbadia a Isola.

Needless to say, cucumber sorbet quickly became a favorite. Its bright, herbal freshness is perfectly balanced with a splash of gin, giving it a sophisticated edge. Whether served at the end of a summer dinner or as a cool afternoon treat, it captures the season's abundance in a spoonful.

Roughly chop the cucumber, collect it in a bowl, and drizzle with lime juice to preserve its bright color and freshness. Sprinkle with the sugar and set aside for 30 minutes.

In a blender, combine the cucumber and the syrup that has formed in the bowl, ⅓ cup/78 ml water, basil and mint leaves, and xantham gum, if using. Blend on high until you get a smooth, vibrant green puree. Pour into a container and let it rest in the fridge for up to 2 hours.

Pour the cucumber puree into your ice cream maker and churn until the sorbet is frozen, thick, and fluffy according to the manufacturer's instructions, usually 30 to 40 minutes.

Because sorbet melts faster than traditional ice cream, transfer the churned sorbet into a suitable lidded container and place it in the freezer to firm up until you're ready to serve.

When ready to serve, scoop the cucumber sorbet into chilled bowls. Drizzle with a splash of gin (if using) and enjoy immediately.

NOTE: If you do not have an ice cream maker, pour the cucumber puree into an airtight container and stash it in the freezer. Every 30 minutes, remove it from the freezer and scrape it with a fork to break up the ice crystals. Repeat this process until the sorbet is smooth, fluffy, and almost completely frozen. It might take up to 4 hours. The final result won't be as smooth as a machine-churned sorbet, but it will still deliver that refreshing, vibrant green flavor. A small amount of xanthan gum goes a long way. In gelato, it works as a stabilizer and thickener, improving its texture, preventing ice crystal formation, and enhancing its creamy consistency. If you cannot find it, just skip it.

Fichi Premurgiani
AZIENDA AGRICOLA
Mena Angela
AZIENDA AGRICOLA
Mena Angela
La Qualità

CILIEGINO
0.65
Sicilia

ACKNOWLEDGMENTS

This book could not have come to life without the love, support, and inspiration of so many people who played a part in its creation.

To my husband, Tommaso—my partner in every sense. Thank you for helping transform ideas into reality, for capturing the beauty of every dish through your lens, for loading the dishwasher more times than I can count, and above all, for always being by my side.

To our daughter, Livia, who lights up our days and keeps us grounded—even in the midst of chaotic recipe testing—and who loves shelling peas and trimming baby artichokes with a focus that would make any cook proud. It certainly makes us proud.

A heartfelt grazie to our family and friends, whose encouragement and enthusiastic tasting turned countless leftover dinners into joyful, rewarding moments.

To my cooking class students and to the wonderful community of Letters from Tuscany on Substack—thank you for your curiosity and your unwavering love for Italian cuisine. Your questions, your stories, your desire to learn: They keep my creativity alive. Your thoughtful feedback—on ingredients, techniques, and even recipe titles—has been truly invaluable.

To the farmers and market vendors who bring the seasons to life on our plates: Your care, your pride, your steadfast dedication to tradition are the heartbeat of Italian cooking.

To my editor, Judy Pray—thank you for believing in this project once again, and for guiding it with such thoughtful care. And to the team at Artisan, who helped turn our vision into something tangible and beautiful.

To Sheela Prakash, a brilliant and talented recipe tester, thank you for your generosity and precision, and for turning every gram and milliliter into cups and tablespoons!

And finally, to you, dear reader—thank you for opening this book and letting me share a part of my world with you. I am sure you will find here many recipes to add to your family cooking repertoire, to bring warmth and joy to your table.

INDEX

Pages numbers in *italics* refer to recipe photos.

T

W

Z

YOUNG FRUIT
ROYAL FRUIT
La Notte

GIULIA SCARPALEGGIA is a Tuscan-born and -bred home cook, food writer, and cooking class teacher. She is the author of seven cookbooks, including *Cucina Povera* (Artisan, 2023). Her blog, *Juls' Kitchen*, was named Best Food Culture Blog by *Saveur* in 2019.

Giulia leads hands-on cooking classes in her family's country home in the heart of Tuscany, where she lives with her husband and photographer, Tommaso Galli, and their daughter, Livia. Through her writing, she shares the everyday beauty of Italian life, from seasonal recipes to heartfelt stories rooted in tradition. Find her on Instagram at @julskitchen and subscribe to her newsletter at lettersfromtuscany.com.

TOMMASO GALLI is a photographer based in the Tuscan countryside, where he lives with his wife, food writer Giulia Scarpaleggia. Together, they run Juls' Kitchen—a family-run food project and cooking school—where he captures the beauty of food, places, and everyday life. He's also the official taster of Giulia's creations. Find him online at @tommyonweb.